PENGUIN CLASSICS

P9-BBN-988

TOMORROW IS NOW

ELEANOR ROOSEVELT's life (1884–1962) spanned the crises the nation faced as it confronted two world wars, the Great Depression, the Cold War, the birth of the United Nations and the human rights movement, and the resurgence of intense debates over civil rights, civil liberties, multilateralism, and feminism. She led an unparalleled public life. Although most well-known for her work as the nation's longest serving first lady (1933–1945), Roosevelt developed a remarkable career in journalism. She hosted political roundtables on radio and for television and delivered more than fifty public lectures a year for more than twenty years. Her nationally syndicated column "My Day" appeared in the nation's newspapers six days a week from 1936 to 1962. A prolific author, she wrote more than 550 articles and twenty-seven books, including a bestselling three-volume autobiography. *Tomorrow Is Now* is her last publication. She was equally active in the diplomatic and political arenas. She served as the only woman member of the United States delegation to the United Nations (1946–1952). As chair of its Commission on Human Rights (1947–1950), she shepherded the drafting and adoption of the Universal Declaration of Human Rights. Her career in politics spanned fifty years and ranged from involvement in early labor and settlement movements to editing state and national Democratic Party publications; from coordinating party outreach to women voters to challenging the party to embrace civil and human rights. As an activist, she worked closely with the National Association for the Advancement of Colored People, the United Nations Association of the USA, and Americans for Democratic Action. She also led a Brandeis University graduate seminar in international affairs, where she urged students to examine both sides of a position, state their position, and act to implement it.

ALLIDA BLACK is executive editor of the fdr4freedoms Digital Initiative (www.fdr4freedoms.org), an educational resource on the life and times of Franklin Roosevelt. She is the editor in chief of *The Eleanor Roosevelt Papers, Volumes I and II: The Human Rights Years, 1945–1948*. She lives in Arlington, Virginia.

WILLIAM JEFFERSON CLINTON was the forty-second president of the United States. Under his leadership, the country enjoyed the longest economic expansion in history. After leaving office, he established the William J. Clinton Foundation with the mission to improve global health, strengthen economies worldwide, promote healthier childhoods, and protect the environment.

ELEANOR ROOSEVELT

Tomorrow Is Now

Introduction by
ALLIDA BLACK

Foreword by
WILLIAM JEFFERSON CLINTON

PENGUIN BOOKS

PENGUIN BOOKS

Published by the Penguin Group

Penguin Group (USA) Inc., 375 Hudson Street, New York, New York 10014, USA
Penguin Group (Canada), 90 Eglinton Avenue East, Suite 700, Toronto, Ontario M4P 2Y3,
Canada (a division of Pearson Penguin Canada Inc.)
Penguin Books Ltd, 80 Strand, London WC2R 0RL, England
Penguin Ireland, 25 St Stephen's Green, Dublin 2, Ireland (a division of Penguin Books Ltd)
Penguin Group (Australia), 707 Collins Street, Melbourne, Victoria 3008, Australia
(a division of Pearson Australia Group Pty Ltd)
Penguin Books India Pvt Ltd, 11 Community Centre, Panchsheel Park, New Delhi – 110 017, India
Penguin Group (NZ), 67 Apollo Drive, Rosedale, Auckland 0632, New Zealand
(a division of Pearson New Zealand Ltd)
Penguin Books, Rosebank Office Park, 181 Jan Smuts Avenue, Parktown North 2193, South Africa
Penguin China, B7 Jaiming Center, 27 East Third Ring Road North,
Chaoyang District, Beijing 100020, China

Penguin Books Ltd, Registered Offices:
80 Strand, London WC2R 0RL, England

First published in the United States of America by Harper & Row, Publishers, Incorporated 1963
This edition with an introduction by Allida Black and a foreword by William Jefferson Clinton
published in Penguin Books 2012

1 3 5 7 9 10 8 6 4 2

Copyright © the Estate of Anna Eleanor Roosevelt, 1963
Introduction copyright © Allida Black, 2012
Foreword copyright © William Jefferson Clinton, 2012
All rights reserved

"Nightmare at Noon" by Stephen Vincent Benet. Copyright 1940 by Stephen Vincent Benet; copyright
1968 by Thomas C. Benet, Rachel Benet Lewis and Stephanie Benet Mahin. Used by permission
of Brandt and Hochman Literary Agents, Inc. Any copying or distribution of this text is
expressly forbidden. All rights reserved.

LIBRARY OF CONGRESS CATALOGING IN PUBLICATION DATA
Roosevelt, Eleanor, 1884–1962.
Tomorrow is now / Eleanor Roosevelt ; introduction by Allida Black ; foreword by
William Jefferson Clinton.
p. cm.—(Penguin classics)
Originally published: New York : Harper & Row, 1963.
ISBN 978-0-14-310699-9
1. United States—Social policy.   2. United States—Relations.   I. Title.
E741.R66 2012
361.6'10973—dc23
2012025137

Printed in the United States of America
Set in Adobe Sabon

Dedicated to
Hillary Rodham Clinton
and
Melanne Verveer
for their unwavering and courageous commitment
to the Universal Declaration of Human Rights

Contents

Foreword by WILLIAM JEFFERSON CLINTON   ix
Introduction by ALLIDA BLACK   xiii

TOMORROW IS NOW

Foreword   3

PART ONE: YESTERDAY

1. We Started from Scratch   9
2. America the Unready   13

PART TWO: TODAY

3. The World Revolution   27
4. The Economic Revolution   34
5. The Social Revolution   50
6. The Revolution in Education   65
7. Getting to Know You   80
8. The Machinery for Peace   96
9. The Individual in the Revolution   110

PART THREE: TOMORROW

10. The Land Is Bright   123

Acknowledgments by ALLIDA BLACK   129

Foreword

When I agreed to provide a new foreword for *Tomorrow Is Now*, I looked forward to reading Eleanor Roosevelt's words again, reliving her passion for social justice and human rights. What I wasn't expecting from her last book, published after her death in 1962, was how clearly relevant it remains to our current challenges at home and around the world. Much of what she has to say about race, poverty, and class; education and the changing workplace; the promise and perils of technology and the need for arms control; the importance of the United Nations, with all its limitations, and the right way for the United States to provide foreign assistance, could have been written this morning. Only an outdated phrase here and there, and the changes of the past fifty years, especially the end of the Cold War and the demise of the Soviet Union, tell us this wise, relevant, hopeful book was written fifty years ago.

Mrs. Roosevelt's concerns about education, for example, could appear as a contemporary op-ed with very few changes—after five decades of stop-and-start education reform. She says the most important thing is to teach children how to think so they can deal with new discoveries and challenges with confidence, embracing change not resisting it. Her description of the far right's simmering anger over social progress and at the 1960 election of John F. Kennedy needs no explanatory footnote for any reader today, nor does her impatience with those who would limit the opportunities for women and girls in the name of tradition.

This said, it would be a mistake to read *Tomorrow Is*

Now and grumble, "Why hasn't anything changed?" Mrs. Roosevelt—born, after all, in the nineteenth century—certainly doesn't. In clear, precise words, she marvels at how far the country has come since her childhood, and urges us to press on. Things have changed for the better, but we must do more, faster. She sees the promise of social innovation in the Peace Corps and the exciting possibilities of the space program, but returns time and time again to how science and technology can be used to advance human dignity and basic rights. How can we use technology to boost world food production and end hunger? How can we protect what works in America while improving what doesn't?

Her focus on practical progress is most striking when she talks about government. At the end of her life she has very little patience for ideology. She's exasperated with the John Birch types she sees yearning for an America based on "rugged individualism"—an idea that she wryly notes has already been obsolete for a hundred years. Americans recovering today from the deepest economic slump since the Great Depression will understand implicitly her meaning when she points out how enlightened business leaders differ from those who fought every advance in our social welfare, from outlawing child labor to the eight-hour workday. Ironically for today's reader, she voices this frustration twenty years before the election of Ronald Reagan and the beginning of the institutionalized antigovernment movement that's now thirty years old and counting.

Regardless of her impatience with the right wing, she can hardly be labeled an advocate of Big Government. When a problem needs a solution, her instinct is to ask how we can build it, manufacture it, farm it, solve it—not how we can legislate it or fund it. She quotes Lincoln to say government's role is to do those things people cannot do for themselves. She clearly believes that includes giving people the tools necessary to succeed and to hinder the tendency of markets to self-destruct. She had good reason to believe in both progressive government and free markets—in 1962, the unparalleled success of the Marshall Plan in rebuilding postwar Europe was still fresh.

In her description of the health-care challenges Americans faced in 1962, before Medicare and Medicaid, there are hints of what she might say about the big challenges we face today. Reading her words, you can imagine her advocating American ingenuity in medicine and in practical hospital and insurance reforms—aided by government—rather than insisting on strictly market-driven or government solutions. And she was a relentless advocate of personal responsibility, so she would tell us that we have to improve our lifestyles. In one of her other books, *It's Up to the Women*, she even included recipes for affordable, nutritious meals.

Those of us who read this book—particularly those with fewer tomorrows than yesterdays—can't help but pick up her essential optimism, even as she laments the roads not currently taken and the uncertainty of the future. Mrs. Roosevelt herself marvels in *Tomorrow Is Now* about what lies ahead, saying, "the greatest and most inspiring adventure of all time probably will be carried out in the next fifty years."

She never envisions America to be in decline, just unready. Her remedy is for us to abandon false security and assume personal responsibility for making positive change. That's what freedom is for.

The next fifty years will be a period of change and challenge even greater than the past fifty, which Eleanor Roosevelt so clearly predicted. Once again, *Tomorrow Is Now*. Once again, we would do well to read the words and embrace the vision of a woman whose life was a precious gift to America and the world.

WILLIAM JEFFERSON CLINTON

Introduction

Eleanor Roosevelt knew she was dying when she began this book. Yet she so wanted to complete it that she endured dangerously high fevers, tremors and persistent fatigue, a raw throat, and bleeding gums to dictate the first draft. Although she eventually yielded to family and friends who pressed her to "slow down" and cancel appointments and public appearances, ER kept working on *Tomorrow Is Now*—even when she grew too weak to hold a teacup and her voice dropped to a whisper. She would apologize to Elinore Denniston, whom her agent had sent to take her dictation, for how much harder it made Denniston's work— especially on those days when ER's voice was so faint that it was almost inaudible. Yet ER continually struggled to make herself heard, pushing herself so hard that Denniston sometimes grew so concerned that she made excuses to cut the sessions short.

Why did ER press so hard to finish this book? She already had a voluminous written record by the summer of 1962. She had written almost thirty books and more than 550 articles. Her nationally syndicated column "My Day" had appeared in papers since 1936, generating a record of more than 8,000 political commentaries. *Ladies' Home Journal* and *McCall's* magazines carried her monthly question and answer column "If You Ask Me" for twenty-one years, leaving more than 250 advice columns for her public to consult. She could have dedicated her last energies to an anthology of her most important works or she could have delegated the task to a trusted confidant to complete after her death. But she did not. She chose to start and finish this book because, as she told Denniston, "I have something that I want terribly to say."[i]

ER firmly believed America's greatness rested upon the power of its ideas, not upon its economic and military might. And now in this new period of dangerous uncertainty, as the world reeled from the atomic bomb, an escalating Cold War, and rapid social, technological, and economic change, it waited "for [America] to provide an example of dynamic drive."[ii] But, to ER's immense frustration, America was sliding downhill at the exact time the world needed America to lead. The nation had abandoned curiosity, sidelined diplomacy, and accepted an outlook governed by fear rather than boldness. It had forgotten that it could set its own course and "make [its] own history."[iii] Its citizens had succumbed to complacency. They either had forgotten or ignored their nation's history—not the dry dates and policies that filled textbooks and encyclopedias, but the daring imagination, boldness, and conviction that had inspired its revolutions against tyranny and slavery and comforted the nation through wars, civil and foreign, and depressions, great and small.

In short, ER contended, America could not lead because it was not ready to lead. For America to regain its leadership and confront the challenges tomorrow presents, "we must learn to think freshly, to re-examine our beliefs, to see how many of them are living and real."[iv] Socratic discussions of politics and governance might make us sound smart, ER wrote, but they could not penetrate our dreams. Americans might be told over and over that we stood on the shoulders of giants, but until we internalized the founders' courage and made it our own, we remained detached observers . . . watching others act for us . . . and ceding control of our hopes and fears to them.

Only a real understanding of the past, ER argued, could give America the insight it needed to summon the imagination, courage, and "high heart" the founders used to create democracy and that which the nation must now use to sustain it.[v] Only when Americans can break free of the restraints fear imposes on their minds and hearts can they be free to find the courage to envision a new world and the skill required to build it.

But as much as this book is about Eleanor Roosevelt's past and the lessons American history taught her, it is about what ER learned from her own observations of politics and policy.

In particular, it reveals how Eleanor Roosevelt could continue to believe in democracy despite almost daily excruciating evidence of its shortcomings and the intense political animosity she encountered day after day throughout her almost-fifty-year career.

Readers accustomed to ER's more famous works—*The Autobiography of Eleanor Roosevelt* or *You Learn by Living*, for example—will meet a different woman as they read this book. She is assertive, direct, and confrontational. She recommends policy and criticizes both political parties. She praises American values while she criticizes American conduct and challenges Americans to abandon the fear and self-absorption she believes undermines the nation.

Some may interpret her dedication to American democracy as simple blind allegiance. Others may interpret her commitment as an act of faith. Cynics may discount it as unthinking liberalism or unquestioned devotion to a progressive past. Liberals may recoil at her unabashed patriotism. All such quick and easy reads not only show little understanding of ER's life, but also overlook her basic point: courage is more exhilarating than fear and in the long run, it is easier.

Tomorrow Is Now is what Eleanor Roosevelt wanted to tell us before she died. It is, she wrote in the foreword: "One woman's attempt to analyze what problems there are to be met, one citizen's approach to ways in which they may be met, and one human being's bold affirmation that, with imagination, with courage, with faith in ourselves and our cause—the fundamental dignity of all mankind—they will be met."[vi]

It is her final and most powerful manifesto.

Eleanor Roosevelt did not have to write this book. She could have sat this battle out. She was seventy-eight years old. She had spent almost fifty years in the political arena, fighting to make America live up to its promise. She had experienced the disappointments of the Progressive era, observed the horrors of two world wars, battled to defend and expand the New Deal, and risked her reputation, her career, and her income, as well as her personal safety, to shepherd the Universal Declaration of

Human Rights to fruition. She had felt that "clutch of fear" in her heart when an assassin's bullet narrowly missed her husband, when her sons and friends went off to war, and when rabid segregationists tried to kill her.[vii]

ER had an unparalleled, complex career. In addition to being the niece of one president, the wife of another, and the nation's longest serving first lady, she had forged a remarkable path in her own right. She had been a teacher, journalist, diplomat, party leader, citizen activist, lecturer, and UN champion. By the time she wrote *Tomorrow Is Now*, she had become democracy's most well-known and outspoken advocate. She may not have had to write this book, but her history and her commitment compelled her to do it. She had come to realize "that nothing of what has happened to me, or to anyone, has value unless it is a preparation for what lies ahead."[viii]

Eleanor Roosevelt could trace her ancestry back to the *Mayflower*. One of her relatives had signed the Declaration of Independence and another oversaw George Washington's inauguration. Her family had money, a fine home, and prominent social status. By the time ER was born on October 11, 1884, happiness had left the family and would not return. Both parents had died by the time ER was ten. Comfort and security eluded her until 1899, when she entered London's Allenswood Academy and encountered its formidable but empowering headmistress, Marie Souvestre. Freed from the social demands her heritage imposed, ER quickly made friends, threw herself into her studies, played field hockey, and strove to overcome depression, self-doubt, and fear. Souvestre, who adored ER and saw a glimpse of the woman she could become, pushed her hard. She demanded that her favorite pupil follow world events and think for herself rather than parrot what she read or heard. She rejected easy answers, demanded well-reasoned and well-documented essays, and sternly rebuked ER when her work did not meet the headmistress's high expectations. As ER later recalled, Souvestre "shocked" ER into thinking, and the teenage ER loved her fiercely for it.[ix]

Family responsibilities arose, and in 1901, ER returned to New York to assume them. Her uncle Theodore was now president, and the pressures on ER to enter New York society intensified. Despair and self-doubt resurfaced, but she dutifully made the rounds of cotillions and house parties. The following year Franklin Roosevelt entered ER's life just as she was trying to balance the independence she learned from Souvestre with the responsibilities her family and her social status required of her. They began courting soon after ER volunteered at the Rivington Street Settlement House and began to investigate working conditions in the garment industry for the National Consumers League. They married March 17, 1905.

Married life was not what ER expected. She had never seen her parents happy and had no idea how to parent, having had very little mothering herself. She knew how close FDR was to his mother, Sara Delano Roosevelt, and hoped that Sara would become the mother she never had. ER did not anticipate, however, that Sara would orchestrate so much of her marriage or control so much of her children's upbringing.

Moreover, ER had eagerly followed FDR to Washington, four hundred miles away from the Roosevelt ancestral home, and had obediently performed the social niceties Washington society expected of a junior cabinet member's wife. Although she hated spending most of her days paying social calls on the wives of her husband's colleagues, she loved being with FDR and thought he was happy. She never expected that just as she summoned the confidence to move away from making house calls and into war relief work, just as she found work that she loved and excelled in, that FDR would fall in love with Lucy Mercer, ER's social secretary.

FDR rejected her offer of divorce. They reunited and strove to build a marriage that was nurturing and empowering for both of them. It was a painful process. They had no models to follow. When the Democrats tapped FDR as their 1920 vice presidential nominee, he asked her to defy tradition and join him on his campaign train. She agreed and soon realized she would spend most of her time on the train alone, as he conferred with aides or addressed voters. FDR's close aide Louis Howe recognized her loneliness, brought her into the campaign, and helped bridge the gap with FDR. When the voters resoundingly defeated the Cox–Roosevelt ticket, FDR and Howe plotted a career that would take FDR to the White House. ER, determined to support her husband's dreams and reclaim her own voice, with both FDR's and Howe's encouragement, divided her time between her family and women's organizations dedicated to the living wage, outlawing child labor, worker safety, and peace.

In 1921, just as ER's burgeoning independence and political activism introduced a different kind of intimacy into her marriage—one in which ER and FDR began to share and confer, strategize and organize—polio redefined their relationship. While FDR battled excruciating pain, knees locked into place like a rusty jackknife, and spiking fevers, ER fought Sara, who repeatedly, and with increasing aggression, insisted that FDR return to Hyde Park, where he could rest and Sara could ensure that no self-centered, crass politician would sap his energy. ER intimately understood how high the stakes were—both for FDR and for herself. If she had not stood her ground, ER later wrote, she would have become "a completely colorless echo of my husband and mother-in-law and torn between them. I might have stayed a weak character forever. . . ."[x]

As FDR concentrated on regaining his physical strength, Howe encouraged ER to resume her political work and to tackle new, more visible assignments. If ER acted as FDR's stand-in, Howe argued, she could draw the party's attention away from his illness and toward the policies and organizational strategies he promoted. All understood that this could also offer ER the independence she cherished.

It was a delicate balancing act. FDR spent a great deal of time out of state, recuperating in the buoyant mineral-rich waters of Warm Springs, Georgia. Although colleagues visited him there, most of his contact with the party was either by letter or by phone. ER dedicated a great deal of her energy to building the party upstate, securing alliances with major labor unions and social reform groups, analyzing legislation for its impact on the state, editing party publications, chairing party committees, and challenging the party to recognize the power and influence of women voters. She entered the national political stage as cochair of the Bok Peace Prize Committee, which organized a nationwide competition for plans to replace the League of Nations, an act that drew the wrath of the isolationist members of the U.S. Senate Special Committee on Propaganda. When radio appeared, ER realized its power to shape public opinion and adjusted her writing and speaking styles to capitalize on the opportunities it presented. Party leaders, such as Governor Al Smith, soon viewed her as an effective politician in her own right. By 1928, when Smith became the Democratic presidential nominee, ER's political ties and the strong leadership she displayed at the state conventions were two of the reasons he tapped FDR as his successor. As Smith confided in an aide, no one was more respected among upstate Democrats than ER.

Yet ER did not limit organizing skills to the New York State Democratic Party. Her political heart lay with the reform groups that directly addressed the issues she thought most threatened Americans: unsafe working conditions, substandard housing, alcoholism, child labor, exploitative wage and hour policies, and war. Rose Schneiderman, the impassioned leader of the Women's Trade Union League (WTUL), and her colleague Maud Swartz, who bore the scars of the Triangle Shirtwaist Factory fire, became ER's tutors and her lifelong friends. ER so valued their insights that she took them to brief FDR on the trade union movement and the specific challenges facing women workers. She embraced the WTUL with fervor, chairing its finance committee, raising funds to pay off the debt on its clubhouse, hosting receptions and picnics for its members, joining its picket lines, and singing its songs: "Though to jail we had to hike, we won the strike. Hurrah!"[xi]

A few years earlier, ER had joined two dear friends from the Women's Division of the Democratic State Committee, Marion Dickerman and Nancy Cook, to create the Val-Kill Partnership to build a small stone cottage on the Hyde Park estate and launch Val-Kill Industries, a job skills program they created to teach furniture making and other crafts skills to local farmers. In 1927, ER invested in and joined the faculty of the Todhunter School where Dickerman served as principal.

As much as she enjoyed her political work, nothing brought

ER more joy than teaching history, civics, and literature to the Todhunter girls. Building upon Souvestre's example, she rejected formality, exuded affection, and demanded that whatever topic her students examine that they consider all points of view. In history class, rather than insisting upon the rote memorization of dates, she expected her students to explore the connection between the past and the present and to "be specific" when supporting their arguments. She worked to "equip them for the coming world" and prepare them to welcome change "rather than fear it." Insisting that girls have the same political education as boys, she made the city her classroom, taking her students to explore courts, settlement houses, police lineups, homeless shelters, and community markets to help them realize how history, literature, and "the seemingly barren study of the machinery of government" were relevant to their lives.[xii]

Thus, by the time voters returned FDR to public service as their governor, ER's multifaceted career was well-established and widely noted by the press, the public, and the party. Although her new position as the state's first lady required a great deal of her time, she reorganized her schedule to meet the expectations she set for herself and those FDR set for her. She split her week in half, spending Sunday night through late Wednesday afternoon in New York City teaching and assisting the WTUL and other organizations she supported, and the rest of the week in Albany hosting receptions and assisting FDR and his team. Her husband might be the governor of New York and as its first lady she was required to resign her positions with the party, but no one was fooled into thinking that ER stored her political acumen in the Executive Mansion's closet— especially since she had consistently argued in print and in person that "women must learn to play the game as men do."[xiii]

As the Great Depression hit New York, ER's dual careers put her in a unique position to observe its devastation and advocate for policies that could alleviate it. The WTUL continually updated her on the conditions "factory girls" encountered, her colleagues with the bipartisan Women's Civic League kept her current on the Depression's impact on the already deplorable housing situation in New York City, and her walks through the city constantly barraged her with evidence of the Depression's wrath. She observed the ever-growing number of soup kitchens and the numbers of men standing in line, waiting for food. She mourned the homelessness that forced New Yorkers to erect Hooverville shanties in Central Park.

In deference to FDR, she no longer addressed specific legislative proposals either before the public or in print. He was the politician now and she remained resolute that there could be only one politician in a family. But she did not abandon her conscience. "I will say what I believe, but I will not stump against my party, regardless of its program," she announced in *Liberty* magazine. "I will not sit on the platform where the subject of the speeches is one upon which I differ with my husband and his party; nor will I issue statements about it."[xiv] She would, however, continue to lobby FDR—but only in private.

ER now focused on swaying the general public instead of elected officials. Rather than lobby or testify before committees, ER used speeches, articles, and the power of her presence to make her positions known. She pressed for action on specific issues rather than specific remedies for specific situations. She told the Brooklyn Unemployment Emergency Committee that the right to work is "fundamental and inherent in our civilization." When people suddenly realize "no work is to be had [it] turns people bitter," and she urged that the distress be addressed immediately.[xv] She told the League of Women Voters of the City of New York charity did not meet the needs of the unemployed, underemployed, and the dispossessed. The situation demanded "something more than temporary alleviation of suffering through emergency aid. . . . It's nice to hand out milk and bread." It makes a person feel good, but it does nothing to "fundamentally" address the causes of the crisis. She urged them to "face the fact" that America was "drifting" its way through the crisis and that it needed to address the change the crisis demanded with open minds.[xvi] When Southern Democratic women asked her if she feared the crisis might make people vulnerable to communism, ER dismissed their concerns. She wasn't "so excited about the Communists," but she was sorely worried about "the growing number of people in New

York who cannot get work."[xvii] When opponents of working women testily argued that working women deprived male breadwinners of an income, ER rose to their defense. Over and over, she urged people to recognize that the unemployed "are not a strange race," that they are just like all of us, only sidelined by an economy they cannot control.[xviii] When people objected, replying that it was not their responsibility, she dismissed their argument. "We are not only part of the government, but we are the government, and on each one of us devolves the responsibility of trying to solve these economic problems."[xix]

In short, by 1932, she had begun to promote the themes that permeate *Tomorrow Is Now*: Fear and suspicion are counterproductive emotions. Charity may satisfy a donor, but it does little to meet the needs of the unemployed or address the underlying causes of their distress. America must be ready to examine different points of view, reject complacency, and embrace change. The government can be only as good as we make it. Interdependence helps sustain independence.

In the twenties, ER found her voice, and FDR and ER found new ways to complement, support, and care for each other. They had battled betrayal and polio, loneliness and despair, in ways that made them more courageous, more hopeful, more skilled, and more independent. They forged a compromise that allowed them to grow into the leaders they wanted to be and the nation needed them to be.

Their compromise worked. FDR supported ER's work and she supported his. But as prospects of his election to the presidency increased, so did her concerns about losing the life she had struggled to create and the responsibilities they both would have to assume. Election eve, after attending FDR's final campaign rally and dining with FDR, Sara, and FDR's trusted advisor Raymond Moley, ER left Hyde Park for New York City at midnight. She would not cancel her Todhunter classes. She loved them too much and FDR's imminent victory meant that she would soon have to quit what she loved doing most. During the two-hour drive back to the city, she confided her concerns to Lorena "Hick" Hickok: "Of course Franklin will do his best if he is elected. He is strong and resourceful.

And he really cares about people. The federal government will have to take steps. But will it be enough? Can it be enough? The responsibility he may have to take on is something I hate to think about."[xx] When reporters pressed her for a comment shortly after his landslide victory, she let her anxieties show. "Of course, I am pleased," she replied. "You're always pleased to have someone you're very devoted to have what he wants." But fully aware of the pressures facing him, she added, "It's an extremely serious thing to undertake . . . the guidance of a nation at a time like this. It's not something you just laugh off and say you're pleased about."[xxi]

Two days later, en route to Albany and the governor's mansion, she let Hick see the depth of her concern. "If I wanted to be selfish, I could wish Franklin had not been elected. I never wanted it, even though some people have said that my ambition for myself drove him on. They've even said that I had some such idea in the back of my mind when I married him. I never wanted to be a President's wife, and I don't want it now." She was "sincerely" happy for her husband. "I couldn't have wanted it to go the other way. After all, I'm a Democrat, too." But, she added, "now I shall have to work out my own salvation."[xxii] She would continue to be "plain, ordinary Mrs. Roosevelt" and accept the criticism her independence incited.

ER spent the four months until FDR's inauguration saying good-bye to the school and the organizations she loved, accepting new assignments, and exploring ways she could be of use to FDR. She agreed to write two books, one of which—*It's Up to the Women*—was a political primer for those who wanted to support FDR's administration. She crisscrossed the country, standing in for her husband and reaching out to women. She gave countless interviews to print and radio news reporters. She told the press that she hoped she could serve as "a listening post" for her husband. The criticism increased.[xxiii]

On Valentine's Day 1933, the Women's Trade Union League hosted a banquet in her honor. More than two thousand attendees jammed the hotel ballroom. After skits teasing and praising ER, she rose to address those who had encouraged and taught her—and serve notice to her critics. Some people had asked her how she dared to speak out, what right she had to present herself "as knowing what other people are going through, what they are suffering." Of course, she admitted, she could not fully understand. "Yet I think I understand more than the people who write me think I do. . . . Perhaps I have acquired more education than some of you [who] have educated me realize. I truly believe that I understand what faces the great masses of people in the country today. I have no illusions that anyone can change the world in a short time. Things cannot be completely changed in five minutes. Yet I do believe that even a few people, who want to understand, to help and to do the right thing for the great numbers of people instead of the few can help."[xxiv]

The next day, as FDR addressed an evening crowd in Miami, an assassin struck. Bullets barely missed FDR and struck four close to him, including Chicago mayor Anton Cermak. FDR was trapped in a convertible, hemmed in by crowds, and totally dependent upon others to move him to safety. Yet he countermanded orders to remove him and insisted that the fatally wounded Cermak be placed next to him in his car and driven to the hospital. His calm astounded his aides, the press, and the public. When ER learned of the attacks, she exuded the same calm. After speaking with FDR, she told the press "he's all right," comforted Sara and her children, and then left, without bodyguards, to give a speech at Cornell.[xxv] FDR and ER were no strangers to assassination. ER's uncle Theodore assumed the presidency after an assassin killed William McKinley, and later TR would survive the bullet wounds a would-be assassin inflicted. Leadership came with risks and they both accepted that.

The Great Depression intensified the winter of 1932–1933 and violence often seemed to lie just beneath the surface. By Inauguration Day, bank failures swept the nation, forcing governors to close the banks in thirty-two states. Half of American mortgage holders feared eviction. Midwest farmers organized to stop foreclosures, threatened auctioneers and bankers who tried to resist their efforts, and organized to block sending their crops to markets. Unemployment officially stood at 25 percent, but was probably closer to 30. Many workers who still held jobs saw their hours cut and their wages decrease. Major charities and some cities declared bankruptcy. Hooverville shantytowns become so prevalent that in some large cities they appeared as cities within cities. Almost a million teenagers became boxcar hobos, seeking sanctuary in freight cars as they rode the railroads from town to town in search of food and work. Hunger marchers trekked to Washington, where they encountered a Capitol surrounded by armed guards. Even Herbert Hoover was frazzled, desperately telephoning FDR at one a.m. inauguration morning.

It was unchartered territory for the nation, not just for the Roosevelts.

ER entered the White House on March 4, 1933. She was forty-eight years old. She had dedicated most of her adult life to reform efforts and, in the process, juggled several different careers. Now as the country faced its most perilous crisis since the Civil War, she had no official position and all her requests to have a clearly defined role had been rejected.

As FDR and his team huddled to address the banking crisis, ER greeted thousands of guests, hung pictures, and moved furniture into the family living quarters. Although thrilled and concerned for FDR, she also increasingly feared that her life for the next four years would be limited to teas, receptions, and ceremonial duties.

On March 6, ER challenged convention and took her first step to defining her new life. She invited forty women reporters, many of whom had covered her during the campaign, to announce that she would "get together" with them regularly. "The idea," she told them, "largely is to make an understanding between the White House and the general public."[xxvi] They could discuss her duties as first lady, but not politics. FDR quickly recognized the potential and, after he proclaimed "that it's time for a beer" and introduced legislation allowing the sale of 3.2 percent beer, referred all questions about beer and the White House to ER.[xxvii]

ER did not extend her ban on politics, however, to "issues." Within the first hundred days, she discussed sweatshops, child labor, rural poverty, higher pay for teachers, and equal pay for women. When a sympathetic reporter warned her that some of her comments might spark a backlash, she responded: "Some-times I say things which I thoroughly understand are likely to cause unfavorable comment in some quarters, and perhaps you newspaper women think I should keep them off the rec-ord. What you don't understand is that perhaps I am making these statements on purpose to arouse controversy and thereby get the topics talked about and so get people to thinking about them."[xxviii] Soon the journalist Bess Furman would quip, "At the president's press conferences, all the world's a stage. At Mrs. Roosevelt's, all the world's a classroom."[xxix]

The male press paid attention, too—especially when in April, FDR and Howe asked ER to visit the Bonus Marchers who had returned to D.C. to lobby the Roosevelt administration to pay out their pensions early. Hoover had infamously sent the army to dislodge the marchers and their families less than a year before; FDR had just secured a stark cut in veteran's benefits as part of his new economic policy; and the first lady would shat-ter precedent, going unescorted into a crowd of protesting men. All recognized the politics at stake as ER tromped through mud to reach the encampment. She greeted as many of the marchers as possible and spent more than an hour hearing about their lives, listening to their concerns, and asking questions. She promised to convey their concerns to FDR. She even joined the men in song. Reporters descended upon the camp, eager to gauge the men's reaction to ER's visit. "Hoover sent the troops," the men told the *Washington Star*. "FDR sent his wife."[xxx] FDR now recognized how powerful an asset ER could become.

ER understood, however, that not all viewed her as an asset, especially when she opposed the Economy Act of 1933 and urged modification to other New Deal policies. But, having discovered how to be herself and help her husband, she dis-counted their complaints. She pushed the National Recovery Administration boards to increase consumer representation. When the Agricultural Adjustment Act required the slaughter of hogs as part of its effort to limit overproduction of farm products, ER convinced the Agriculture Department to distrib-ute the meat to the hungry and dispossessed. Working closely with Molly Dewson, director of the Women's Division of the

Democratic State Committee, she succeeded in securing a record number of senior appointments for qualified women—and
defended qualified, committed Republican women, e.g., the
Children's Bureau's Grace Abbott, from dismissal. When FDR
empowered Harry Hopkins to create the Civil Works Administration, ER, who deeply cared for and respected Hopkins,
pressed Hopkins to fund She-She-She camps, Civilian Conservation Corps camps for women. A few were created, not
enough, but ER took great pride in them. FDR had discounted
her strong objection to the dismissal of married women working for the federal government. Now, at least one part of the
administration addressed the plight of unemployed women.

ER had always cultivated her own sources of information. In
New York, she relied on the reports and other materials she
gleaned from her work with reform groups, her own observations and letters and phone calls from colleagues and friends.
She soon realized that to help the New Deal she would have to
resurrect and expand that network. She suggested that Hopkins hire Hickok, who had resigned her position with the Associated Press because she had fallen in love with ER and could
no longer cover her objectively, to travel the nation and report
on the conditions she saw and on the effectiveness of New Deal
programs. The reports Hickok sent to FDR, Hopkins, and ER,
as well as the personal letters she sent to ER, convey in dispas-
sionate but vivid terms the Depression's impact on rural and
urban communities.

ER also saw firsthand how people struggled to maintain
their self-respect amid deprivation. Having proved to FDR
with the Bonus Encampment that serving as a "listening post"
could help secure popular support for the New Deal, she
embraced a travel schedule that amazed the press and others
not familiar with her stamina. In four months, she traveled an
unprecedented 40,000 miles, by car, rail, and—the newest
and riskiest venue of transportation—air. She insisted that no
Secret Service accompany her, arguing that she did not need
protection and that the agents would prevent the conversations she traveled to have. Merging formal visits and receptions with inspections of soup kitchens, schools, public

works projects, homeless shelters, shanties, hospitals, jails, and farms, ER honed her own understanding of the Depression's devastation. She observed how race interfered with relief, how the problems the Southern farmer faced differed from those encountered by her neighbors in upstate New York, and how people struggled to maintain their pride in such dire climates. When she returned to D.C., the *Washington Post* headlined its story "First Lady Spends Night in White House."

Americans had already begun to share their plight with ER, but when ER entitled her first article for *Pictorial Review* "I Want You to Write to Me," 300,000 Americans responded in four months. These letters—and the millions she received throughout her twelve years in the White House—became her lifeline to the American public. Her correspondents often revealed themselves to ER as they had never done to anyone before. They sent her notes scribbled on dirty brown paper bags, stationery, and notebook paper. One woman in desperate need of diapers and a baby blanket sent her engagement ring as collateral. Others ranted against FDR and accused ER in exceedingly personal terms of destroying the nation, undermining women, and abusing children. ER embraced these letters—fifty of which she would answer after midnight when she could finally settle into a quiet space. They were her direct line to the hearts and minds of the American people—evidence of the American psyche, the expectations the nation set for the Roosevelt administration—and an ever-present, inescapable reminder of the responsibilities she and FDR had assumed.

The letters reinforced the conversations she had and the observations she made as she traveled the nation. She could not help but reflect upon her own encounters with fear, embarrassment, and disappointment and the solace, courage, and independence she gained from those who helped her rebuild her life. Many Americans now blamed themselves, others blamed the government, many lost the courage to struggle, and some simply resigned themselves to a life of sadness and want. The biggest challenge confronting the nation, ER intuited, was the Depression's potential to separate us from one another and from the government. The only way to combat this, ER believed, was for Americans to recognize their "inter-dependence" without forsaking their independence. As *Tomorrow Is Now* proves, ER would spend the rest of her life challenging America—and, later, the world—to recognize that "one part of the country or group of countrymen cannot prosper while the others go downhill, and that one country cannot go on gaily while the rest of the world is suffering."[xxxi]

This was not an easy position to maintain. By 1935, as the Second New Deal began, ER had seen some success, only to have the administration walk away as a final push was needed or politics intervened and the political capital she needed was expended for another project.

After the 1934 midterm elections, ER remained hopeful that the Senate would finally endorse U.S. membership in the World Court. She continued to speak out in support of the World Court and had contributed an article to Carrie Chapman Catt's recently released *Why Wars Must Cease*. But isolationist Democrats joined their Republican colleagues to rail against it. The charismatic radio priest Father Charles Coughlin led a nationwide campaign to protect America from the World Court judiciary, who "are philosophically and nationally prepared to gang us into submission." Their "crude internationalism and their unsound love of minorities," he proclaimed, "would destroy American independence" and "enmesh [Americans] with the debasements of the standardized poverty of Europe."[xxxii] The night before the Senate was to vote on ratification, ER took to the airwaves to rebut Coughlin. NBC had just aired Senator Robert Reynolds's (D-N.C.) floor speech opposing ratification when ER strode into the studio. She spoke, she told her audience, as "a citizen and a woman deeply interested in these issues." After refuting Coughlin's points, she stated: "The only real question before us now is whether we want to throw the weight of the United States behind cooperative efforts of nations to develop international law and apply it to the settlement of disputes or whether we despair of any substitute for war."[xxxiii] Ratification fell seven votes short of the two-thirds majority necessary to ratify a treaty. ER and FDR were enraged.

ER devoted more of her time to Arthurdale, a Subsistence

Homestead project for unemployed miners living in unfathom-
able rural poverty in Reedsville, West Virginia, than she did to
any one specific endeavor. She often drove up from Washington to inspect construction, visit schools, attend square dances,
and spend time with families she had befriended. She pressured Harold Ickes and Rexford Tugwell to release funds to
help resettle and retrain the miners and construct homes with
indoor plumbing, so residents would not have to walk through
snow and rain to use the outhouse, bathe, or wash their dishes.
She recruited the financier Bernard Baruch to help fund
schools and other structures. But she and Baruch failed to persuade industry to relocate to Reedsville, and government interest, always sporadic at best, rapidly declined and eventually
the government liquidated its investment.

As FDR prepared to submit his second wave of legislation to
Congress, ER worked to support his initiatives and to address the
concerns of those left outside the first New Deal—unemployed
youth; artists, writers, musicians; and African Americans.

Many unemployed young people had never seen capitalism
work. Some had seen their family farms disappear in the twenties. Others saw an erratic industrial economy yank their
fathers like yo-yos. ER recognized that Hitler rode into office
on the backs of the Hitler Youth, and, as she told the press, "I
live in real terror when I think we may be losing this generation. We have got to bring these young people into the active
life of the community and make them feel that they are
necessary."[xxxiv] She invited student groups, influential publishers, and men FDR respected to her New York City apartment
to marshal support for the program that would become the
National Youth Administration (NYA). She also pushed hard
to have African Americans included in the program and championed Mary McLeod Bethune's appointment to direct the
NYA's Minority Affairs division.

Art, ER declared, "expresses what many of us felt in the last
few years but could not possibly have either told or shown to
anyone else." Artists had the power to depict what "we ordinary people feel but can't reveal" and, thus, could help depict
our fears as well as our dreams.[xxxv] Insisting that art was not

only a national pastime, but a tool necessary to sustain democracy, ER goaded FDR into creating the Federal Art, Theatre, Dance, and Writers' Projects. She defended the work when censors and critics tried to shut it down, dismissing their complaints targeting "radical" content. Some painful things must be discussed, ER replied. Moreover, art did not tell us what to think; it encouraged us to think for ourselves, to explore new ideas, and to appreciate our relationship to one another.

After Subsistence Homestead officials denied African Americans' admittance to Arthurdale, ER invited NAACP executive secretary Walter White and the presidents of African American universities to the White House to discuss the situation. Their watershed conversation, which lasted until midnight, quickly became a tutorial on racial discrimination. She pressured the National Recovery Administration to investigate wage discrimination and challenged the navy's practice of confining African American sailors to mess hall duty. She spoke out against lynching and the poll tax and forcefully supported increased funding for African American schools. She regularly visited African American schools, churches, and community centers. She used her column to stand with Marian Anderson when the Daughters of the American Revolution denied her use of Constitution Hall and deftly drew the nation's attention to the inherent hypocrisy of discrimination.

Aryanism increased her disgust with American racism. Americans, she told an interviewer, wanted to talk "only about the good features of American life and to hide our problems like skeletons in the closet." Their refusal to address prejudice fueled racial hostility. Americans must confront their bias, recognize "the amount of intimidation and terrorization" it fosters, and stop such "ridiculous" behavior.[xxxvi] As America debated how best to protect its democracy against a probable Axis assault, ER urged the nation to recognize that a true democracy must include all Americans, regardless of race.

The more outspoken ER became, especially about race relations, the more intense her critics became. Republicans and Southern Democrats distributed campaign buttons mocking her. A few FDR advisors feared that she could jeopardize his election to a historic third term. J. Edgar Hoover plotted to strip her of her citizenship and send her to Liberia. Death threats escalated.

The brutality of the impending world war gravely concerned ER, who well remembered the soldiers and veterans she met and the war-scarred communities and ravaged fields she saw when she accompanied FDR to post–World War I France, and the intolerant reaction it inspired at home. She chafed at the limits the administration and Congress imposed on immigration and refugee policy, chaired the Committee for the Care of European Children, and gave visible support to refugee organizations. She advised FDR to issue the executive order banning discrimination in war-related manufacturing work and pressed reluctant manufacturers to comply with the law. She pushed women to join civil defense work, to enlist in the military, and to "build morale and help others."[xxxvii] When FDR began to implement internment, she appealed for calm and worked, without success, to dissuade him from relocating Japanese Americans.

Convinced that the lesson of World War I was that America won the war only to lose the peace, she celebrated and promoted the principles FDR enshrined as the Four Freedoms: freedom of speech and information, freedom of worship, freedom from want, and freedom from fear. She hoped that FDR's production policy would not only supply the material the Allies needed to defeat fascism, but also lay the groundwork for a more robust and just society. Her efforts to promote this, coupled with her refusal "to put the New Deal away in lavender," often made her the target of intense hostility—as when the nation's press blamed her for the 1943 Detroit race riot.[xxxviii]

ER had pressed FDR to let her visit troops in the Pacific so that they might receive the attention the war columnist Ernie Pyle brought to soldiers fighting in Europe. After "the Negro situation became too hot," FDR let her go.[xxxix] What she saw in those five weeks would tear at her conscience forever. She walked more than a hundred miles of hospital corridors, spending hours with severely wounded men. She witnessed the horrors of mash units; talked with scared, war-scarred, and homesick soldiers; and walked the burned, raped landscape.

"The war fills me with the greatest sense of responsibility I dread I will never be able to discharge," she wrote a friend. "Oh Lord," she prayed, "lest I continue in my complacent ways help me to remember that someone died for me today. And help me remember to ask and to answer, am I worth dying for?"[xl]

She returned home, determined to redouble her efforts to honor the sacrifice she saw. More and more she turned to "My Day" to describe the sacrifice of combat in ways she hoped would help Americans overcome the fear and grief the war injected into their lives. She urged them with increasing passion to assume the courage a world grounded in the Four Freedoms required. Within the White House, she served as a back channel to FDR for aides who feared the war secretaries would subvert FDR's plans to abolish the colonial mandate system, and followed FDR's proposal for the United Nations with keen interest. She looked forward to accompanying him to San Francisco, where representatives from fifty-one nations would draft the United Nations Charter.

FDR's sudden death from a cerebral hemorrhage in April 1945 stunned and saddened ER, and forced her, once again, to reorder her life. Rather than a celebratory cross-country trip with FDR, she had to bury him, leave the White House, settle the estate, and cope with the knowledge that her daughter had recently facilitated Mercer's return into FDR's life. She followed UN developments from afar, listening to opening sessions over the radio, reading news accounts, and exchanging detailed letters with Secretary of State Edward Stettinius. She resisted pressures to run for office, accept a cabinet position, or manage a political action organization. When Ickes traveled to Hyde Park to ask her to reconsider, she told him that it was her children's turn in the political arena and that she felt "very strongly" she could be more useful in other ways. The moment she accepted a party position she "would have to follow the party line pretty consistently," and although she wanted to work with and for Democrats, she thought the "knowledge that I will be free of any obligation may at times be healthy." Don't worry, she promised, with her column and her lecture tour, "My voice will not be silent."[xli]

By the fall, frustrated by Truman's inconsistent position on full-employment and wage, rent, and food control policies, ER had reentered the political debate. She used "My Day," public lectures, and keynotes at fund-raising dinners to oppose loyalty oaths and escalated Cold War rhetoric and pronouncements by the House Committee on Un-American Activities that not only violated her politics but also threatened the interdependence America had adopted to win the war. Repeatedly she told her audiences that American domestic policies had huge international implications: "We are in an important moment in history," she told a Boston gathering. "What happens here in the United States will either give courage to people in the other parts of the world, or on the other hand, will sap their courage."[xlii] In New Jersey, she declared that "we must have confidence in one another and must avoid a situation where everybody approaches everyone else with suspicion."[xliii] "It takes just as much determination to work for peace as it does to win a war," but, as she confessed to a Chicago audience, she wondered "if we're going to have the courage and the strength to sustain our effort to win the peace."[xliv]

Thus by late December 1945, when ER accepted Truman's invitation to join the first U.S. delegation to the United Nations, she had reasserted her voice, made her positions clear, and decided on a new political path. She did so, she told her readers, because "I feel a great responsibility to the youth who fought the war. . . . Everyone of us has a deep and solemn obligation to them which we should fulfill by giving all that we are capable of giving to the making of peace so they can feel that the maximum good has come from their sacrifice."[xlv]

ER entered the United Nations in January 1946 unsure of her role, convinced that her importance only lay in her status as FDR's widow. She carried the pressure of being the only woman on the delegation, the only non-lawyer, and the only member without a college education. Yet by the time she left the UN seven years later, she would do so reluctantly, having developed an international reputation in her own right as a skilled debater, a shrewd negotiator, and the United Nation's most indefatigable advocate. In short, ER's tenure at the UN changed her. She grew tougher, bolder, more conscious of her power and influence, and deeply troubled by the horrors she had seen in the Pacific and the political intransigence she encountered.

Initially, the male leaders of the U.S. delegation did not know what to do with ER and thought if they could park her on the Social, Humanitarian Cultural Affairs Committee, she could work on issues they considered inconsequential. They focused their energies on structuring the Security Council and regulating atomic weapons. They were, therefore, blindsided when the care and feeding of sixty million European displaced persons surfaced as a contentious issue and when the Soviets used the debate surrounding the continuation of the United Nations Relief and Rehabilitation Administration to challenge the anticommunist West. When the Soviets continued to exploit the issue, the delegation had no choice but to turn to ER, who understood the political and humane issues involved, to refute the Soviet demand for repatriation. Her gracious dismantling of the Soviet position stunned her colleagues and led John Foster Dulles to confess, "I feel I must tell you that when you were appointed I thought it was terrible and now I think your work has been fine!"[xlvi]

ER, pressured by the U.S. Army, would soon tour a displaced persons camp for Jewish, Polish, and Baltic refugees. She did not want to go because she knew she would be haunted by what she saw and heard, but she felt compelled to investigate. She heard the stories of the survivors of the Nazi concentration camps and the pleas of Jewish survivors to immigrate to Palestine. She talked with non-Jews displaced for political and economic reasons. What she saw emboldened her in ways she had not anticipated. While still there, she used "My Day" to convey angst and outrage. With "an aching heart," she asked, "when will our consciences grow so tender that we will act to prevent human misery rather than avenge it?"[xlvii]

Convinced that America had been "spared for a purpose" from the destruction that the war inflicted on other nations, ER seized all avenues at her disposal—columns, speeches, articles, private conversation, radio broadcasts, newsreels, and correspondence—to urge Americans to recognize what was at stake and to assume both the responsibility and the financial cost of world leadership. Fervently, she repeated that Americans must learn that "you cannot live for yourselves alone. You depend on the rest of the world and the rest of the world depends on you."[xlviii] UN debates on the refugee crisis, the Geneva Conventions, atomic energy, arms control, the proposed UN peace force, the creation of Israel, the implementation of apartheid, the demise of colonialism, and women's rights underscored to ER the crying need for America to accept its connection with the rest of the world—and how crucial a commonly shared vision could be in overcoming the haunting legacy of war.

ER hoped that the Universal Declaration of Human Rights (UDHR) would provide that vision. The General Assembly had voted to establish the United Nations Human Rights Commission (UNHRC) and instructed it to create an international bill of rights. The UNHRC promptly elected ER its chair and expected her to oversee all the tasks associated with creating the document and securing its adoption by the United Nations General Assembly.

The battle to create an international vision of human rights drew on every skill ER possessed—and challenged her in ways she never envisioned. As the talks began, ER saw that any discussion of human rights quickly became ensnarled in Cold War politics. Deeply worried that escalating political tensions could easily spark another world war, ER decided to push for comprehensive agreement that could be adopted as quickly as possible. A fearful world, still recovering from the worst war in its history, needed a vision sooner than it needed a treaty. Thus, she urged that the UNHRC's assignment be divided into three complementary tasks: drafting a declaration of human rights, conceptualizing a covenant of human rights, and designing a human rights court that could hold violators accountable. Convinced that Truman would not be elected, and that she would not be reappointed to the United Nations, she strove to have a declaration adopted by the end of 1948.

Drafting the Universal Declaration of Human Rights required monumental effort. The world had never agreed on a common concept of rights, and now it had to do so in the shadow of unimaginable horror and economic uncertainty. As chair of the UNHRC, ER had to create a climate where all the eighteen member nations—each of whom was represented by a very vocal representative instructed to follow the parameters his/her government set for the declaration—could envision, debate, and articulate rights. Ultimately, she would chair more than three thousand hours of contentious debate to define human rights and whether they applied to all men, women, and children everywhere—regardless of race, religion, ethnicity, nationality, age, country of origin, income, and social status. What did the right to work, the right to wages and income, the right to assemble, the right to food and shelter, the right to education, the right to health, the right to dissent, the right to vote and participate in government, the right to nationality, and the guarantees against torture and discrimination mean? What was the philosophical basis for human rights? What did the guarantee of equal treatment in one's community or government or workplace mean in different political systems? What made a human rights violation so egregious that the offending nation's sovereignty could be challenged? How were women's human rights to be protected? Moreover, as chair of the drafting committee, ER had to make sure that the vision she guided the committee to create was presented in clear, readily comprehensible, and empowering prose.

ER considered the adoption of the Universal Declaration of Human Rights her most important work. It is also the starkest example of her political acumen, her stamina, and her vision. As the UDHR took shape, she had to convince a reluctant, if not outright resistant, State Department to accept a definition of human rights that included social, economic, and cultural rights rather than just civil and political rights. Then she had to persuade the Soviets, whom she increasingly distrusted, to not sabotage the committee's work. No one other than ER could have negotiated this minefield. The Secretary General and the General Assembly appreciated her skill, and, as she finished her remarks urging the UDHR's adoption, the delegates rose in tribute, giving her the first standing ovation in UN history.

Outside the UN, she traveled the world as the UN's unofficial roving ambassador. At home, she promoted popular support for the UDHR with the energy and shrewdness she displayed in securing its adoption. She debated critics representing the American Bar Association, Senator John Bricker and his strident anticommunist colleagues, and American segregationists. She devoted countless hours to the United Nations Association of the USA, helping it build local chapters, and using her lecture tours to urge Americans to assess the UN for themselves rather than simply absorb anti-UN propaganda.

ER's commitment to the United Nations did not derail her commitment to combating the politics of fear and urging democratic reform at home. She continued to oppose loyalty oaths, the Smith Act, and the House Un-American Activities Committee. She gave very public support to Dean Acheson, Alger Hiss, Dorothy Kenyon, and other associates when zealots questioned their patriotism. She helped found the leading liberal think tanks of the postwar era: Americans for Democratic Action and the National Issues Committee, and campaigned for those Democrats she thought honored the Four Freedoms.

But the campaign for racial justice still remained her domestic priority. She joined the boards of directors of the National Association for the Advancement of Colored People (NAACP) and the Congress of Racial Equality (CORE). By 1950, she championed integrated schools, housing projects, labor unions, and neighborhoods. By the mid-fifties, she moderated civil rights platform hearings at Democratic national conventions, advised candidates and civil rights organizations on ways to mobilize their constituencies, and continually used her column and lecture tours to educate a recalcitrant public on the inherent dangers of a racist society.

Now completely comfortable in her own limelight, ER challenged average Americans to follow her lead and attacked politicians who protected their careers at the expense of American justice. Impatient with the politics of avoidance, ER perfected her own version of the politics of confrontation and urged Democrats to keep what her husband called its rendezvous with destiny.

As she aged, she no longer concealed her bitterness when Democrats refused to address fear and racial prejudice. When she learned Senator James Eastland had offered his home to those who would resist school desegregation and incite racial violence, she let disgust permeate her column. "I could hardly believe that our country would allow such a man to lead and that our people would allow themselves to be guided by such ideas and such untruths." "We say that democracy is inspired by Christianity" yet the nation allows Eastland to use the Bible to justify "doctrines entirely opposed to the whole spirit of Christianity, or ethics, of human brotherhood." Such behavior depressed her immensely. "I do not have to go South for sorrow. I sorrow here for the shame of our past three years."[xlix]

Such outspoken bitterness had its personal costs. The Scripps-Howard newspaper chain instructed all affiliates to drop "My Day." Segregationists in Guilford, North Carolina, dynamited a tree not three hundred yards away from the church in which she spoke. The Houston White Citizens' Council demanded she cancel her lecture and leave Texas "immediately" and, when she refused, hurled racial epithets at those attending the event and threatened to run her out of town. Later that year the Ku Klux Klan, with the support of the county sheriff, planned to raid the Highlander Folk School the day ER was scheduled to appear. When the FBI informed her about the potential attack, she refused to cancel and drove unescorted on dark mountainous roads. When its attempt to capture ER failed, the Klan put a $25,000 bounty on her head.

While ER rejoiced in John Kennedy's election in 1960, the early sixties did not offer her much hope that America would change. The politics of fear still appeared to govern international as well as domestic policy—with devastating consequences. The Bay of Pigs invasion solidified Fidel Castro's control over Cuba, fostered a refugee crisis that state and federal officials did not know how to address, undermined the Kennedy administration's Alliance for Progress, and set the stage for the Cuban Missile Crisis. The construction of the Berlin Wall, coming less than three months after Kennedy's summit with Nikita Khrushchev, gave irrefutable evidence of Soviet encroachment. The qualifications the administration set for accepting child refugees from China made her "cringe."

"People who are fleeing starvation may, I think, be slightly difficult to identify as 'desirable' and 'undesirable,'" she wrote in "My Day," "and who knows whether a baby is going to be 'desirable' when it grows up."[l] Even her dear friend Adlai Stevenson's appointment as U.S. ambassador to the United Nations could not offset the growing concern she felt for the UN as senators threatened to withhold America's dues and the State Department refused to push for the International Covenant on Civil and Political Rights and the International Covenant on Economic, Social, and Cultural Rights. All too often the "super-patriotic anti-Communist groups" stoked just enough fear to delay the change she thought essential.

Attacks targeting African American students enrolled in New Orleans public schools "appalled" her, as did assaults on two African American undergraduates attempting to attend the University of Georgia.[li] The "deplorable" drive-by shootings of two African Americans trying to register to vote in Fayetteville, Tennessee, and the imprisonment of students in Rock Hill, South Carolina, enraged and depressed her.[lii] The beatings of the Freedom Riders and African American students distributing leaflets in Birmingham so angered her that, despite a spiking fever, she traveled to Washington to chair a mock trail of their assailants, "one of the most difficult experiences" she had ever been through. She "found it difficult—and intolerably painful—to accept the fact that things [like this] could happen here in the United States. This was the kind of thing the Nazis had done to the Jews of Germany."[liii]

She urged Americans to appreciate that "in a very real sense, the United States is the world's show window of the democratic process in action." "What people see when they look in that window" determines not only their attitude toward the United States but also their assessment of democracy in action. And now ER bemoaned, "the stubborn ignorance of large groups of our own citizens, which have led to injustice, inequality, and sometimes, brutality" is what many "people see when they look in that window." America increasingly appeared "unready" to address the challenges "the era of world revolution" presented it.[liv]

ER's despair did not make her question democracy, human rights, or the American dream. It did, however, lead her to question how committed political parties, the federal and state governments, and average Americans were to taking the bold steps necessary to concretize these abstract ideas. It goaded her to fight harder to preserve and instill these values.

When college students asked why she could continue to defend democracy when democracy had lost its spark, she urged them to realize their own power to reclaim democracy. "It depends on what each of us does," she insisted. "What we consider democracy means and what we consider freedom in a democracy means and whether we really care about it enough to face ourselves and our prejudices and to make up our minds what we really want our nation to be, and what its relationship is to be to the rest of the world. The day we know that then we'll be moral and spiritual leaders."

She knew how hard this work would be. She had done it, but she wanted them to do it too. "You are going to live in a dangerous world for quite a while I guess, but it's going to be an interesting and adventurous one." She was old, growing tired, and needed help. She wanted them to harness their passion and help build a nation grounded in human rights. She challenged them to reject fear and accept the challenge of building a more just society. She wanted them to develop "the courage to face it and . . . the courage to face [themselves]." Only then, she told them, would they have the "imagination and understanding" they needed to risk themselves for a true peace.[lv]

ER saw *Tomorrow Is Now* as her last chance to continue this conversation. She could not rest until she said it. She refused to accept that fear could overshadow courage and that democracy had lost its power to inspire. She did not want to die thinking America had sidelined its vision. So she fought her tuberculosis long enough to summon the strength to issue a final call to action.

As ER declared in *Tomorrow Is Now*, "Staying aloof is not a solution; it is a cowardly evasion."[lvi]

ALLIDA BLACK

NOTES

i Eleanor Roosevelt, *Tomorrow Is Now* (New York: Harper & Row, 1963), ix.

ii Eleanor Roosevelt, *Tomorrow Is Now* (New York: Penguin Classics, 2012), 23.

iii Ibid., 10.

iv Ibid., 23.

v Ibid., 4.

vi Ibid., 5.

vii Eleanor Roosevelt, Pan American Coffee Hour, December 7, 1941, Speech and Article file, Anna Eleanor Roosevelt Papers, Franklin D. Roosevelt Library (AERP). The transcript as well as transcripts of "My Day" and several articles cited in this introduction may be found online at the Eleanor Roosevelt Papers Project Web site (www.gwu.edu/~erpapers), referenced in these notes as ERPP.

viii Roosevelt, *Tomorrow Is Now*, 3.

ix Roosevelt, "Seven People Who Shaped My Life," *Look* 15 (June 19, 1951): 54–56, 58. See also ERPP.

x Cited in Joseph P. Lash, *Eleanor and Franklin* (New York: W. W. Norton and Company, 1971), 276.

xi Brigid O'Farrell, *She Was One of Us* (Ithaca: Cornell University Press, 2011), 5.

xii Eunice Fuller Barnard, "Mrs. Roosevelt in the Classroom," *The New York Times*, December 4, 1932.

xiii Roosevelt, "Women Must Learn to Play the Game as Men Do," *Redbook* magazine 50 (April. 1928): 78–79, 141–42.

xiv Roosevelt, "How to Choose a Candidate," *Liberty* 9 (November 5, 1932): 16–17.

xv "Job Relief Delays Charged to Hoover," *The New York Times*, January 20, 1931.

xvi "Charity Not Enough, Says Mrs. Roosevelt," *The New York Times*, January 13, 1932.

xvii "Mrs. Roosevelt for Wider Culture," *The New York Times*, March 4, 1930.

xviii Eleanor Roosevelt, "The Unemployed Are Not a Strange Race," *Democratic Digest* (June 1936): 19.

xix "Mrs. Roosevelt Urges Courage in the Crisis," *The New York Times*, January 15, 1932.

xx Lorena Hickok, *Eleanor Roosevelt: Reluctant First Lady* (New York: Dodd, Mead and Company, 1962), 55.

xxi "Wife of Roosevelt Is Not 'Just Pleased,'" *The New York Times*, November 9, 1932.

xxii Hickok, 1–3.

xxiii "Mrs. Roosevelt Plans to Keep in Touch with the People from the White House," *The New York Times*, January 22, 1933.

xxiv "Women Poke Fun at Mrs. Roosevelt," *The New York Times*, February 15, 1933.

xxv "Mrs. Roosevelt Takes News Calmly," *The New York Times*, February 16, 1933.

xxvi Eleanor Roosevelt Press Conference, March 6, 1933, Bess Furman Transcript, in Maurine Beasley, *The White House Press Conferences of Eleanor Roosevelt* (New York: Garland Publishing, Inc., 1983), 7.

xxvii Kenneth S. Davis, *FDR: The New Deal Years, 1933–1937* (New York: Random House, 1979), 63,

xxviii Emma Bugbee interview quoted in Lash, 363.

xxix Bess Furman, *Washington By-Line* (New York: Knopf, 1949), 194.

xxx "Mrs. Roosevelt Leads Song at Bonus Camp," *The Washington Post*, May 17, 1933.

xxxi Roosevelt, *Women's Democratic News*, December 1932, and Lash, 383–384.

xxxii "Coughlin Renews World Court Fight," *The New York Times*, January 28, 1935.

xxxiii "First Lady Urges World Court Step," *The New York Times*, January 28, 1935.

xxxiv *The New York Times*, May 7, 1934.

xxxv Roosevelt, "The New Governmental Interest in the Arts" in *American Magazine of Art*, 1943, 47.

xxxvi Ralph J. Bunche, "Memo on Interview with Mrs. Franklin D. Roosevelt at the White House, May 15, 1940, quoted in Allida Black, *Casting Her Own Shadow: Eleanor Roosevelt and the Shaping of Postwar Liberalism* (New York: Columbia University Press, 1996), 89.

xxxvii Roosevelt, Pan American Coffee Hour, December 7, 1941, op. cit.

xxxviii Roosevelt, "Freedom of Speech," October 14, 1941, broadcast, Tape File, Speech and Article File, AERP.

xxxix "The Reminiscences of Henry A. Wallace," August 18, 1953, Columbia Oral History Office, quoted in Black, 92.

xl Quoted in Lash, 654.

xli Roosevelt to Harold Ickes, May 26, 1945, in *The Eleanor Roosevelt Papers, Volume I*, ed. by Allida Black (Charlottesville: University of Virginia Press), 36.

xlii "Mrs. Roosevelt in PAC Talk Here," *The Boston Post*, November 1, 1945, in *The Eleanor Roosevelt Papers, Volume I*, 125.

xliii "Suspicion as Peace Bar Feared by Mrs. Roosevelt," October 2, 1945, in *The Eleanor Roosevelt Papers, Volume I*, 111.

xliv Roosevelt, Founder's Day Dinner Address, Roosevelt College, November 10, 1945, in *The Eleanor Roosevelt Papers, Volume I*, 137.

xlv Roosevelt, "My Day," December 22, 1945.

xlvi Roosevelt to Joseph P. Lash, February 13, 1946, in *The Eleanor Roosevelt Papers, Volume I*, 249.

xlvii Roosevelt, "My Day," February 16, 1946.

xlviii Roosevelt, Address to Women's Joint Congressional Committee, March 14, 1946, in *The Eleanor Roosevelt Papers, Volume I*, 274.

xlix Roosevelt, "My Day," April 27, 1957.

l Roosevelt, "My Day," May 25, 1962.

li Roosevelt, "My Day," January 1, 1961.

lii Roosevelt, "My Day," January 4, 1962.

liii Roosevelt, *Tomorrow Is Now*, 52.

liv Ibid., 27, and "My Day," April 30, 1962.

lv Roosevelt, "Freedom and Human Rights," in *Courage in a Dangerous World*, ed. by Allida Black (New York: Columbia University Press, 2000), epigraph.

lvi Ibid.

Tomorrow Is Now

There were many men and women who hesitated, in Holland, appalled at the dangers of the long journey to America, frightened by the risks involved in a new and uncivilized country, dismayed at the prospect of facing the unknown.

"It was answered, that all great and honorable actions are accompanied with great difficulties and must be enterprised and overcome with answerable courages. It was granted the dangers were great, but not desperate. The difficulties were many, but not invincible. For though there were many of them likely, yet they were not certain. It might be sundry of the things feared might never befall; others by provident care and the use of good means might in a great measure be prevented; and all of them through the help of God, by fortitude and patience, might either be borne or overcome."

WILLIAM BRADFORD, *OF PLYMOUTH PLANTATION*

Foreword

'Tis dangerous to take a cold, to sleep, to drink; but I tell you, my lord fool, out of this nettle, danger, we pluck this flower, safety.

SHAKESPEARE

In the past I have written of the era in which I grew up and of the experiences which shaped my life, from a lonely childhood in a caste-bound society with narrow traditions, through the crowded years of my husband's Presidency, in which a great depression and a major war brought sweeping changes to the whole world; and finally, of the years in which I came to know a great part of that world at first hand and, through my work with the United Nations, to learn that its destiny, like the tainted winds now blowing over it, is common to all.

More recently, I tried to set down in *You Learn by Living* what I had reaped from that long and varied experience.

Now, however, I have come to see that nothing of what has happened to me, or to anyone, has value unless it is a preparation for what lies ahead. We face the future fortified only with the lessons we have learned from the past. It is today that we must create the world of the future. Spinoza, I think, pointed out that we ourselves can make experience valuable when, by imagination and reason, we turn it into foresight. It is that foresight we must acquire. In a very real sense, *tomorrow is now*.

So, while this is a book about today as it will affect and shape tomorrow, it is also a book about yesterday, about our beginnings, about the history of the great nation we carved out of a wilderness, about the qualities of the men and women who made that history. Above all, it is a reminder that we do make our history, that we are making it now—today—by the choices that shape our course.

It is essential that we remind ourselves frequently of our past history, that we recall the shining promise that it offered to all men everywhere who would be free, the promise that it is still our destiny to fulfill. But to fulfill that promise we must be ready, like the men who signed the Declaration of Independence, to pledge our lives, our sacred honor, and all our worldly goods.

It is essential to turn back to our history now and then to remind ourselves of the principles on which this nation is based, to read once more the Declaration of Independence and the Bill of Rights. There are people who claim that, today, the Bill of Rights would never get out of committee. I cannot accept so shameful a suggestion; we must turn back to re-examine our faith and see that, once again, we make it bright and strong.

It is essential that we cast out fear and face the unknown, as our ancestors faced the unknown, with imagination and integrity, with courage and a high heart.

It is essential that we re-examine our country and our world and their relationship; that we reconsider our personal strength as well as our political and military strength, and see how they affect each other.

It is essential, above all, that in making history we do not forget to learn by history, to see our mistakes as well as our successes, our weaknesses as well as our strengths.

In this book I want to talk to that spirit of America which is in each of us. But it is to the young, particularly, that I want to speak; to remind them of the background of our nation; to remind them that we could never have conquered the wilderness, never have built the foundations of a country and a new concept of life, based on the fullest and freest development of the individual; never have overcome vast difficulties and dangers, if we had not had a new idea, an idea so noble in concept that it gave us confidence in ourselves and gave us the strength to build this new nation, step by step.

Once more we are in a period of uncertainty, of danger, in which not only our own safety but that of all mankind is threatened. Once more we need the qualities that inspired the development of the democratic way of life. We need imagination and integrity, courage and a high heart. We need to fan the spark of conviction, which may again inspire the world as we did with our new idea of the dignity and the worth of free men. But first we must learn to cast out fear. People who "view with alarm" never build anything.

I have seen, over and over during recent years, the results that have come in Israel because the young were fired by the idea of building a new country. Here in America, I would like to see our people fired by the vision of building a new and a peaceful world.

In the following pages I have set down one woman's attempt to analyze what problems there are to be met, one citizen's approach to ways in which they may be met, and one human being's bold affirmation that, with imagination, with courage, with faith in ourselves and our cause—the fundamental dignity of all mankind—they will be met.

E. R.
Hyde Park
August 1962

PART ONE

YESTERDAY

Not for the past alone—for meanings to the future.

WALT WHITMAN

I.

WE STARTED FROM SCRATCH

They that can give up essential liberty to obtain a little temporary safety deserve neither liberty nor safety.

BENJAMIN FRANKLIN

Not long ago, during one of the many uprisings of colonial peoples against their masters, a disgruntled Englishman declared, "That damned American Revolution is still giving us trouble."

Yet, as I have lectured around the country addressing groups of students, I have become increasingly appalled to discover that comparatively few of them have any sound knowledge of American history. Few of them have any clear understanding of the world wars in which we have been engaged, of the great depressions through which we have passed. Fewer still are familiar with the background of the Constitution, the Bill of Rights, the Declaration of Independence.

Not long ago, a boy in a high school in South Carolina referred to our Constitution as "that unknown document." Within the past few months a group of college students were given a list of statements and asked whether they approved of them. To a man the students rejected them. Only then were they told that the statements composed the Bill of Rights. They had not even recognized them! That means that they had never been taught about the conditions in the Old World which led to the creation of the Bill of Rights for the protection of the basic liberties of the American people.

Certainly we are not going to be able to defend our American institutions if our young people do not understand what they are, why they are, and what makes them essential to the maintenance of freedom and human dignity.

One thing I believe profoundly: *We make our own history.* The course of history is directed by the choices we make and our choices grow out of the ideas, the beliefs, the values, the dreams of the people. It is not so much the powerful leaders that determine our destiny as the much more powerful influence of the combined voice of the people themselves.

Look back at the American continent of the seventeenth century: primeval forest, gigantic mountain ranges, turbulent rivers, vast plains, savage animals, and even more savage men. A land that had remained basically unchanged from the beginning of time.

That was what our ancestors faced after the terrors of a long and dangerous sea voyage, sailing away from the only world they knew, the only way of life of which they had any experience, sailing into the unknown, the unforeseeable. But they brought with them courage and hope; they brought determination and a vision of a better life; they were fired by a desire to create a new kind of civilization, without fear or oppression, where men could develop freely and fully their best abilities and capacities. They brought with them, too, faith in Christian justice and in a system of equitable law.

And, because they believed in these things with all their hearts, they planted them in the new soil, where they flourished, and built a new world. They made their own history.

There were mistakes, of course. The creation of something new under the sun must always suffer to some degree from the process of trial and error. But, almost from the beginning, the nature of this new structure began to fire the imagination of the world. It became apparent that, with sufficient courage, with undimmed faith in their values, men could create a world of freedom and justice in which to live.

At first, this was a small stone flung into the world's pool of thought, but the ripples widened and spread. The farthest ripples are still touching peoples remote from us not only geographically but in their degree of civilization. As the unhappy Englishman said, the reverberations of the American Revolution are still being felt.

That brave voyage into the unknown was only the beginning, of course. The newcomers did not stop with creating a new kind of government and a new way of life. They were not willing to confine the great adventure to the eastern seaboard. They set out to explore and tame a continent, to tunnel its mountains and bridge its rivers, to make its land yield food and its forests provide shelter.

In covered wagons they moved ever westward, always into the unknown, the unforeseeable. The journey was dangerous. Daily life was dangerous. For a woman, isolated from her kind, to bear a child was dangerous.

But their courage and their faith bore fruit. The pioneer was no longer alone. Small settlements grew to towns and then to cities. In time, the most powerful and prosperous nation the world had ever known stretched from ocean to ocean.

From the beginning, the differences between the New World and the Old were apparent. Other lands were, for the most part, inhabited by more or less homogeneous populations. But our own country soon became one of mixed peoples. In spite of this fact—as I am constantly discovering with surprise—a number of people still think of the United States as being overwhelmingly English, Protestant, and white. This erroneous idea influences their whole outlook.

The truth is that, *by the time of the American Revolution,* over half the population was probably non-English. By then, indeed from the time of the settlement of the thirteen colonies, one of the most obvious facts was the wide diversity in religion, from the Puritans to the Quakers, from the Catholics to the Jews, from Roger Williams to the Calvinists.

It was this enormous diversity in religion, in race, in cultural background that contributed most to our unique development. It provided a richness and variety of texture. It sparked new ideas. And it was the flowering of those new ideas that led to the American Revolution.

It was John Adams who said, "The American Revolution

was effected before the war commenced. The Revolution was in the minds and hearts of the people."

I am stressing this overwhelming power of ideas because of my firm conviction that it is the force of ideas rather than the impact of material things that made us a great nation. It is my conviction, too, that only the power of ideas, of enduring values, can keep us a great nation. For, where there is no vision the people perish.

With the American Revolution the stone was thrown into the pool. For the first time colonies had freed themselves from their mother country. The ripples began to spread. What one people could do another could do. So, one by one, other colonial peoples began to throw off their shackles, to set themselves free.

Today, less than two hundred years later, the ripples have washed the farthest shores. Colonial peoples everywhere have chosen independence. And, as they begin to build anew for themselves, country after new country has used our American Constitution, at least in part, as its model. Since the end of World War II, seven hundred million people have discarded colonialism; one out of every four persons in the world. That is a very big ripple.

2.

AMERICA THE UNREADY

There are certain words,
Of our own and others', we're used to—words we've used,
Heard, had to recite, forgotten . . .
Liberty, equality, fraternity,
To none will we sell, refuse or deny, right or justice.
We hold these truths to be self-evident.

I am merely saying—what if these words pass?
What if they pass and are gone and are no more,
Eviscerated, blotted out of the world? . . .

They were bought with belief and passion, at great cost.
They were bought with the bitter and anonymous blood
Of farmers, teachers, shoemakers and fools
Who broke the old rule, and the pride of kings . . .
It took a long time to buy these words,
It took a long time to buy them and much pain.

STEPHEN VINCENT BENÉT,
"NIGHTMARE AT NOON"

After the Civil War, which at last made a reality of the phrase, "one nation, indivisible," an odd thing happened. As a handful of men began to make great fortunes, the voice of the people as a whole began to be disregarded. It is not pleasant now to look back at that era of exploitation when not only the vast resources of the land but human resources, as well, were sruthlessly used. Shortly before the beginning of the twentieth century nearly two million young children, many of them only ten years old, labored for all the daylight hours.

Men became so absorbed in short-range goals and immediate personal gain that they failed to see beyond their own noses. They lost sight of the broader picture. That, too, is a part of our history.

Sometimes I wonder why we remain, as a people, so persistently blind to lessons of our own history. Many years ago, at the beginning of the Spanish-American War, my uncle, Theodore Roosevelt, spoke with exasperation about "America the Unready." His complaint then was that we were about to engage in a war for which we were totally unprepared.

Did we learn from this experience? The answer is to be found in the length of time it took us to prepare for the two great world wars.

This same persistent short-sightedness shows up in any study of our depressions. In 1836, in 1857, in 1873, in 1907, and in 1929 the country suffered economic collapse. Each time the pattern was repeated. Each time a shaken and outraged people was taken completely unaware. Each time the typical newspaper comments, like these examples from the year 1837, were repeated:

"It cannot be disguised that we have over us a worse tyrant than any of the Caesars."

"For six years our country has been the theater of experiments unprecedented in their character and extremely dangerous in their results."

And each time there were the glowing promises of future unparalleled prosperity; the threat that, if changes were made, grass would grow in the city streets. But once any of these depressions ended, its lessons were forgotten. The next economic cycle again found America the Unready.

The building our ancestors constructed with trial and error has provided a hope and a beacon everywhere for men who would be free. And yet—how are we defending that structure today? What steps are we taking to protect it? What plans have we made to modernize it so that it will be strong enough to withstand the storms of the future? It is time—time now—to make the dwelling sound and tight. Not one of us can afford to shut his eyes, to turn away, to say, "This does not concern me."

One reason, I think, that we have tended, as a people, to ignore the forecasts of bad weather ahead is that for us in general the sun still shines brightly. Our people, aside from occasional bad pockets of poverty, are the best off in the world. Why then, they wonder, must they bestir themselves?

Yet here, too, they could learn by our history, by that despairing cry of George Washington when he was trying to shape an army in spite of the general lethargy of the people: "It is among the most difficult tasks I ever undertook in my life to induce these people to believe that there is, or can be, danger till the bayonet is pushed at their breasts."

What causes this persistent blindness, this stubborn refusal to recognize the inexorable force of change in the world? I find it difficult to accept the fact that the descendants of men and women who created a brand-new society have grown resistant not only to change itself but even to accepting the fact that change exists. What inhibits so many of us from recognizing our present situation as it is, from defining our problems clearly, and from seeking a solution that is suited to the structure of our modern world?

One reason for this situation, it seems to me, is that we have a small but noisy body of men and women whose knowledge of American history appears to have stopped with Washington's Farewell Address. Now we are all united in honoring the courage and integrity of Washington. But surely no one can seriously take the position that political ideas suited to a struggling young nation, shut off from the world by wide oceans and connected to it only by leisurely sailing ships, apply with any validity to a powerful nation conditioned to men in orbit and a world that can be encircled in minutes.

This seems as pointless as to suggest that we revert to the horse and buggy because Washington traveled that way; that we live in the isolation of self-sustaining farms where people did everything for themselves, from spinning the thread for clothing to preparing their own medications, because life at Mount Vernon had to be lived that way.

The extreme right wing in American politics today appears to be trying to project itself into this obsolete background. It operates on the theory that American history has stood still, that the world has stood still, that it is possible to revert to the conditions of a long-dead past.

Let us consider for a moment how dead that past actually is. We can do so by taking a look at some recent history. The end of World War I found us a dominant world power. Our territory was unscathed. Our loss in manpower was slight compared to that of most of the European combatants. Our economy was strong.

With the end of World War II, we emerged as the strongest nation in the world. Again, we were alone in having no territorial devastation. Again, though our manpower loss was heavy, it was proportionately lighter than in other countries. Again our economy was strong. We were able to convert quickly to peacetime conditions. We had a backlog of economic needs and a backlog of savings with which to satisfy them. Wartorn Europe turned to us, because it had nowhere else to turn for its needs. And—we had the Bomb. We were, we thought, invulnerable.

But what happened in the next decade? We no longer controlled the secret of the Bomb. For Americans it now constituted threat as well as promise. And other drastic changes had taken place. We had won World War I, we thought, but 200,000,000 Communists followed in its wake. And after World War II there were 900,000,000 more Communists. Today, one out of every three persons in the world is a Communist or, at least, lives under Communist domination.

Evidently, we are living in a rapidly changing world. And there is no going back. For some people, of course, there is a nostalgic charm about certain ideas of the past. That idea of rugged individualism, completely divorced from the public interest, for example. It has a heroic sound, a kind of stalwart simplicity. The only trouble is that for many years it has been inapplicable to American life.

Back in 1914, Elihu Root, a Wall Street corporation lawyer, Secretary of War under McKinley and Secretary of War and State under Theodore Roosevelt, addressed the New York State Bar Association. This was fifty years ago. At that time, he was trying to point out that *for the fifty years before that* the world of the rugged individualist had been as dead as the dodo in America and it was high time people recognized the conditions under which they lived. A short time ago, a friend sent me a copy of this speech. In the light of recent events he felt that I would find it interesting. I did:

The real difficulty [Mr. Root said] appears to be that the new conditions incident to the extraordinary industrial development of the last half-century are continuously and progressively demanding the readjustment of the relations between large bodies of men and the establishment of new legal rights and obligations not contemplated when existing laws were passed or existing limitations upon the power of government were prescribed in our Constitution.

In place of the old individual independence of life in which every intelligent and healthy citizen was competent to take care of himself and his family, we have come to a high degree of interdependence in which the greater part of our people have to rely for all the necessities of life upon the systematized cooperation of a vast number of other men working through complicated industrial and commercial machinery.

Instead of the completeness of individual effort, working out its own results in obtaining food and clothing and shelter, we have specialization and division of labor which leaves each individual unable to apply his industry and intelligence except in cooperation with a great number of others which activity conjoined to his is necessary to produce any useful result. Instead of the give-and-take of free individual contract, the tremendous power of organization has combined great aggregations of capital in enormous industrial establishments working through vast agencies of commerce and employing great masses of men in movements of production and transportation and trade, so great in the mass that each individual concerned in them is quite helpless by himself.

The relations between the employer and the employed, between the owners of aggregated capital and the units of organized labor, between the small producer, the small trader, the consumer, and the great transporting and manufacturing and distributing agencies, all present new questions for the solution of which the old reliance upon the free action of the individual wills appears quite inadequate. And in many directions the intervention of that organized control which we call government seems necessary to produce the same result of justice and right conduct which obtained through the attrition of individuals before the new conditions arose.

I have quoted Mr. Root's comments both because they represented—a half century ago—the point of view of a man whom no one has ever called a radical, and because the ideas that seemed fifty years out of date to him then are still held tenaciously today by a vociferous group of people who persist in the belief that the United States and the world have remained basically unchanged since the colonies became a nation.

What makes this pathetic wishful thinking dangerous is that constant attempts are made to apply it to the foreign policy of the United States, to domestic policies, to our national defense, to our economy, to widespread social conditions, to education.

To me, one of the strangest features of the extreme right wing position is that its chief rallying cry is its bitter opposition to Communism. In fact, many of these well-meaning people seriously regard themselves as the sole defenders of the American way of life. And yet there are curious parallels between the objectives and the methods of the right and the left; there are a growing number of situations in which these extremes meet.

Let's take the matter of objectives first. Among the demands of the right wing are: "Let's get rid of the United Nations. . . . Let's throw out the Peace Corps. . . . Let's forget about the starving of the world and take care of our own country first. . . . Let's withdraw from our dealings—particularly economic aid—with those who are seeking to establish a new and better way of life for themselves elsewhere."

These are all things that the Communists are trying their best to force us to do!

But even more serious than the curious coincidence of objectives between right and left is the strong similarity in the methods that are often employed by both sides. For instance, we have long known of the Communist technique of establishing small cells in universities, businesses, labor unions, whose job it is to attract other people and fire them with a desire to serve the cause. How many people are aware of the cells established in much the same way by the Birchites? These, as a rule, are heavily financed and they often have an appeal to the young who like to be different in groups but have a terror of being different by themselves.

Not long ago, I had a rather amusing experience when on a lecture trip. The chancellor of a southwestern university, a man of great wisdom, was approached by one of his students, a young Birchite.

"We intend to picket Mrs. Roosevelt's lecture tonight," he said.

"Dear me," the chancellor replied mildly. "Do you know her subject?"

"No. But she is a controversial figure and a university is no place for controversial ideas."

"She is speaking on how best to fight Communism."

"Well?"

"Well, you see," the chancellor pointed out gently, "with your ideas of guilt by association, if you picket her for speaking against Communism, you will have aligned yourself, by your own logic, on the side of Communism."

That night there was no picket line.

The least amusing part of this story, of course, is that terrifying conviction that "a university is no place for controversial ideas." Here, indeed, right and left wing meet in perfect harmony. To the Communist-trained youngster, of course, there are no controversial ideas to be found in a university. He is told what to believe and there is no possible discussion. The mind is not trained—it is merely shaped.

Another meeting of the extremes appears in the method of intimidation. I am not suggesting, of course, that drastic forms of punishment or violent threats are applied in this country. Methods like that can be dealt with promptly by exposure to public opinion. The pressures here are generally exerted by the power of money.

It is a pleasant thing for a group to find itself lavishly financed. It is unpleasant to be warned that you must not deviate or the financing will be cut off. But worse, in these days of growing conformity, is the threat that if you deviate in your thinking you will be different from your colleagues, your fellow workers, your fellow students, your contemporaries. And that is intolerable to a number of people. A group has solidarity. An individual alone has only his courage and his integrity.

We cannot turn back to a past historical era and attempt to live there, as Mr. Root pointed out. What we need from our past history is to learn its lessons, profit by our mistakes, analyze our successes, find out all that it has to teach us.

One day, some years ago, Max Lerner asked me to talk to a senior class at Brandeis University in a course he had instituted. Its purpose was to familiarize his students with various phases of their own world, both in the present and in the past. He asked me to talk to these young people about the world of my childhood, fifty years ago.

That look backward was as revealing to me as it was to the students. What they learned from that talk—which extended from a lecture to a question hour and then into further questions and talks that evening and the following day—I do not, of course, know. But I am clear about what I learned. In retracing the physical life of my childhood I was reconstructing from memory a way of life that had vanished from the earth. A life without faster transportation than a horse and buggy; without faster communication than newspapers; without labor-saving devices or such mass concepts as housing developments and shopping centers.

All this seemed remote enough, but attempting to reconstruct the way people had thought and acted in that period a half century away was almost impossible. The youngsters at Brandeis were as alien to that world as Mark Twain's Yankee was to King Arthur's Court.

That experience proved to be valuable for me. Since then I have often wondered how many people over the age of, say, fifty, try to reconstruct their past in the light of today. Only by doing so can one form a sharp picture of a changing world, and of the changes one has had to make oneself, no matter how painfully or reluctantly, to adjust to that world.

Looking back now, one can see how many mistakes could have been avoided, how much progress could have been made, if the people of my generation, for instance, had looked clearly at their contemporary world, analyzed what they saw, wondered about its meaning not just for their own time but for the future. Suppose we had asked ourselves: "What is the meaning of the increased use of machinery? Where will it eventually lead us? What problems will it create? How will it affect people for good and for bad? How can we prepare for these changes?"

Unhappily, we didn't take a clear look. And today we are once again America the Unready. This time it matters more than it has ever done before.

We started from scratch, every American an immigrant who came because he wanted a change. *Why are we now afraid to change?* How can we regain our sense of boldness in the face of danger, of imagination to create new solutions, of courage and high-heartedness in carrying them out?

It is obvious that if we keep turning back we'll never move forward, and the new world will leave us behind. The arch conservatives want a shrinking and not an expanding America, with its sphere of influence ending at its own doorstep. And yet it must be plain that our world leadership may go by default if we practice nonintervention, or if we concentrate merely on fighting the Communists within, or if we continue our static thinking.

In a sense, nearly all great civilizations that perished did so because they had crystallized, because they were incapable of adapting themselves to new conditions, new methods, new points of view. It is as though people would literally rather die than change. Sometimes, seeing the stubborn resistance of large groups of Americans to accepting the existence of totally new conditions, their determination to meet the future as though it were the past, I am deeply puzzled. How did it happen that a people with constantly developing ideas on methods of production and distribution appears unable to develop new ideas, new points of view, new solutions to the problem of adjustment to change?

There are no easy answers in the back of the book, no antecedents to fall back on; but the founders of our nation had no precedents to fall back on either. What they did have, and may we be ever grateful, was courage, self-confidence, and the willingness to face the unknown and shape it according to their dreams. Surely we have not so watered down that courage and confidence and boldness that, to cling a little longer to our illusory tranquillity, we will surrender our leadership, our bright vision.

We cannot deny that the choice is to be made. We must not forget that the choice must be made now.

Changes are coming upon us—and upon the world—at so fantastic a pace that there is no time to waste. The Bomb, nuclear power in all its manifestations and potentialities, automation, the exploration of outer space, the presence of men in orbit—these no longer are limited to the science pages of the papers. These are the conditions that have provided a scientific revolution. Unless we are to find ourselves at a hopeless disadvantage we must recognize their existence, must acknowledge that they are altering the face of our world, and plan ahead intelligently to master their use before they can destroy us.

For on our ability to meet the challenge depends the future of America, probably the future of the world. *Is it to be* The Waste Land *or* The Good Earth?

The world is waiting for us to provide an example of dynamic drive, a bold reaffirmation of the values on which our nation was founded. Staying aloof is not a solution; it is a cowardly evasion. I wonder if this movement of passive withdrawal from the world is not a sign that, in some of our people, at least, the old values, the courage, the deep-seated faith in the cause of the freedom of man have lost their bright image.

Before we can meet successfully the challenge of the world, the challenge of tomorrow, we must learn to think freshly, to re-examine our beliefs, to see how many of them are living and real.

PART TWO

TODAY

Long, too long America,
Traveling roads all even and peaceful you learn'd from joys
   and prosperity only.
But now, ah now, to learn from crisis of anguish, advancing,
   grappling with direst fate and recoiling now,
And now to conceive and show to the world what your
   children en-masse really are.

WALT WHITMAN

THE WORLD REVOLUTION

To fight out a war, you must believe something and want something with all your might. So you must do to carry anything else to an end worth reaching. More than that, you must be willing to commit yourself to a course, perhaps a long and hard one, without being able to foresee exactly where you will come out.

OLIVER WENDELL HOLMES, JR.

This is the era of world revolution. On every continent revolutions are going on. Some of these are political, some are economic, some are ideological. There are revolutions of backward peoples and revolutions of poor peoples—not always the same thing. There are revolutions of men seeking economic security and revolutions of men seeking a political voice in their government, again not always the same thing.

Whatever the land, whatever its degree of civilization or economic stability, whatever the source of its immediate protest, there is implicit in all these revolutions the basic aspirations of all men for freedom of the human spirit, for the expression and recognition of their human dignity—that fundamental hunger which the institutions of the United States were designed to satisfy.

And yet, as we watch the course of those revolutions, we become uneasily aware that, in many cases, once independence has been achieved there follows a period of letdown. Self-government, the building of every institution from the ground up, providing trained men, establishing some form of self-protection from hostile nations and ideologies, looms as a gigantic and frustrating task for peoples who have had no background of training in citizenship.

So they look, inevitably, toward the land which first established proof that colonies might be free. They want guidance and encouragement and understanding help—without the kind of interference that we ourselves would never tolerate. And so far they find chiefly an ambivalent attitude, a lack of direction in our thinking about these new lands, a shilly-shallying way of saying: "Will we—won't we?"

In the space of half a generation the face of our world has changed. The old landmarks are gone. Governments are gone. Ways of life are gone. And through the scientific discoveries that have been revealed, one after another, new worlds, new ways of life are beginning to emerge. Today, men are exploring outer space. They have unleashed the unknown immeasurable power for good or for evil. And that power is here to stay.

Most of us, whether dimly or vividly, have come to recognize this revolutionary force as it finds expression around the world: in the Far East, in India, in Africa, in South America.

What most of us have failed to recognize is the dominant fact of our own country. We, too, are living through a revolution. In fact, we have been feeling its impact with increasing force during the past ten years. It is high time that we discover our own revolution, understand what it is doing to us, and its implications for the future.

Of course, there is a general awareness that for a decade we have been going through a scientific revolution. But what we have failed to grasp is that *if you have a revolution in one area, it is bound to affect all the other areas*.

Our scientific revolution has inevitably had and will continue to have a revolutionary effect on our economy. That revolution in our economy is causing a social revolution. That, in turn, is bringing irresistible pressures to bear, which will—which must—affect our whole approach to education.

How does it happen that we have not already faced this tremendous upheaval, this revolution which, while not filled with bloodshed as in some in other lands, is equally far-reaching?

The chief reason, I think, is fear. Change means the unknown. It means being jolted out of a rut that has grown comfortable and familiar from long residence. It means, too many people cry, insecurity.

Nonsense! No one from the beginning of time has ever had security. When you leave your house you do not know what will happen on the other side of the door. Anything is possible. But we do not stay home on that account. After all, the man who cowers under a tree in a storm, thinking that he is secure, merely runs more risk from the lightning.

The time has come for us to cast off our fear like a wornout garment. It clouds the judgment. It paralyzes action. Causes for fear? Of course there are. But there always were. We fear the Bomb—and rightly. But for hundreds of years the hapless peoples of the world were threatened by forces that were, at that time, completely beyond their control: by the Black Death, which killed one out of four in Europe, year after year; by cholera and smallpox and pestilence.

Today, we are free of those fears because we have learned to understand them and to eliminate their causes. Now we have the knowledge of the Bomb, knowledge with which we could destroy our civilization, and we are afraid. But action is better than the paralysis of fear. We have to learn to think freshly about our new revolutionary world, to free our intelligence from the shackles of fear, and set it to work on the most challenging problem we have ever faced: the preservation of our civilization.

To no generation has such a challenge been given. With courage and faith, with intelligence and the free use of the mind in tackling new problems, we can meet it greatly.

In my opinion, the American people were thrown off balance by the Russian launching of the first space missile. Since then, we have been following the development of Russian science, especially in outer space, with a kind of dread. People say, "They are ahead of us." And they are afraid. They lose sight of the fact that in most fields the Soviets lag far behind us. Indeed, when we shift our attention from men in orbit and potential journeys to the moon we are clearly aware that there are few ways in which the Soviets have been able to meet the challenge of the democracies here on earth.

Later, I shall take up, one by one, the areas in which the Soviets have failed—and continue to fail—to achieve the results that they have so long promised their people. But first I want to discuss the ways in which this new scientific revolution has been used to shift our attention away from our own strength and our own purposes to focus it instead on Soviet activities in outer space.

As I go around this country and the world, talking to large groups of people, I am struck by the repetition of the same questions, over and over. People ask: "What is Khrushchev doing? . . . What is he planning? . . . Does he do this better? . . . How can we rival him or surpass him?"

Instead of that, I would like to hear the voice of the American people ring out loud and clear, proud and self-confident, saying: "This is what we are doing. This is what we believe. This is the kind of world we want. This is the kind of world we intend to work for."

Because, and never doubt it, given a chance to see both sides honestly, all men who care about freedom will know where they belong.

But what has been our answer to the challenge of nuclear power, which has revolutionized our world? We are continuing to experiment with nuclear testing. Because of the mutual distrust that exists between the two great powers we take turns setting off greater and greater explosions, in the oldest and most futile form of international politics, the age-old struggle to maintain a balance of power.

In making this momentous decision, of course, the President of the United States has little choice. By his oath of office he is obliged to accept the terrible risk; otherwise he would be endangering the national security. The pressures are overwhelming to keep our knowledge a little ahead of what our scientists believe the Soviets have achieved.

As far as the lay mind can see, this senseless and literally deadly competition can go on *ad infinitum*. But at some point, as more people acquire the same information, there may be an accident. Who can be sure that, on some occasion, some youngster may not make a mistake? Radar is a wonderful thing, but it is sometimes difficult to interpret what is seen on the screen. So even the controls themselves can prove to be fallible.

And meantime, even without this major catastrophe, *what may we be doing to the human race?* Unfortunately, we know more about nuclear power than we do about the effects of fall-out. But it is possible that we are continuing to pollute the air dangerously, to condemn who knows how many unborn children to malformed bones.

We are disturbed, and rightly so, because a few thousand babies have been crippled by a dangerous drug. Yet we have not expressed the same indignation, we have not made the same determined effort to prevent the condemnation of infinitely more children by this insane arms race. The present situation puts every human being in the world in constant potential danger, every day of his life.

Now the madness in this lies in the fact that we do not want a nuclear war. Just as certainly, the Soviets do not want one. There is no victor in such a war; there is only destruction on a world-wide scale.

The Bomb will be something to live with as long as mankind exists. We have to learn to cope with it before it is too late. That means we have got to learn to change our thinking, to look afresh at the new elements in our world, and find new ways to deal with them. Since we do not have another Benjamin Franklin, who could look at everything in his world freshly, we will have to learn to be our own Franklins. But while we wear the handcuffs of fear we are not free to consider the ultimate choices or their meaning.

There is no conceivable excuse for a great nation like ours being carried along helplessly on "the wave of the future." We can decide the direction of our own course. We must—now— turn our imaginations toward the area of what can be done, concretely, to meet this problem and prevent total destruction. We know that the continuation of a race between the United

States and the USSR in continued tests of greater or less power can lead nowhere but to ultimate disaster.

It is curious that after the first stunned horror of Hiroshima, after mankind's first shock of realization that an evil genie had been released, a kind of apathy descended. Like the grape growers who live on the side of Vesuvius year after year, knowing that periodically the volcano will erupt and their vines, their homes, their families may be consumed in burning lava, people settled back, with a fatalistic shrug, as though to say, "It's very tragic, but, after all, what can we do about it?"

So the scientific revolution hit the United States as it hit the rest of the world. And we began to sustain a number of other shocks. This was, after World War II, to be a world that would cooperate for its mutual benefit; a world that, sick of bloodshed and destruction and hatred, would live at peace. With the threat of Nazi conquest vanquished, all would be well.

Was it? Instead, we found a divided world. One part of that world was quite sure that its beliefs must be accepted by all mankind or otherwise, as they put it, "the law of the future cannot be carried out."

One of the first steps taken by the Soviets to implement this policy was to train scientists. But this was a new kind of scientific training. In the past, scientists had been educated with a view to seeking and sharing knowledge. These men, however, were attempting, for purely military reasons, to control the knowledge discovered, from time to time, in other parts of the world.

Within an incredibly short period, partly by the use of defecting scientists from the West, the Soviets shared the grim knowledge of the Bomb. From that time on, we have been at an impasse. Neither side dares unleash nuclear warfare; each side, to maintain the precarious balance of power, continues to test.

I have no more trust in the Soviet leaders than any other person, but I think we must give them credit for a certain amount of common sense and self-interest. Their people are paying a heavy toll in sacrifice of comforts, even in daily necessities, to maintain their heavy armaments program. For involved in this insane death struggle is an incalculable amount of money.

The United States is also putting vast sums of money into military developments and experimentation. It is true that we have a great deal of money. It is also true that most of us have not as yet felt the drain in our daily lives to any great extent. But in countries that are today beginning from scratch, as the Soviet Union did forty years ago, and Red China is doing now, this drain is felt.

Think of what we could do if we were—all of us—to channel these vast sums of money into other fields! We could eliminate pockets of poverty. We could improve health and education. If this is true for the United States how much more must it apply to developing countries, or countries with old civilizations that they are having to modernize in order to meet the more modern countries on an equal basis.

Without further delay, we must face the implications of our scientific revolution and evolve workable plans for directing its course.

4 ·

THE ECONOMIC
REVOLUTION

Life does not give itself to one who tries to keep all its
advantages at once. I have often thought that morality may
perhaps consist solely in the courage of making a choice.

LÉON BLUM

With the onset of a scientific revolution, repercussions began
almost at once to be felt in other areas. The one in which it
was felt most sharply, the one that perhaps affects the American people most closely, is the area of economics. The upheaval
there has already changed the old patterns, led to the discard-
ing of old methods.

At the same time, of course, the entire world has been going
through an economic revolution—from the newest countries
in Africa to the old established order in Western Europe. The
strange and, to me, disconcerting element about this is that the
United States with its vaunted know-how has been so much
slower than most countries in facing and acknowledging the
fundamental changes that have come about.

Where we have lagged behind is in facing the facts of our
industrial revolution, in familiarizing ourselves with the problems and in using our know-how to provide answers to the basic
problems. Certainly our economic revolution should be easier to
cope with than that of countries which generally lack the sim-
plest tools. But what are we doing about it? For the most part,

sticking our noses in the sand and pretending that we can go on as we are, drifting, without meeting our problems head-on.

It is fairly well recognized, I think, that here in America we are in need of complete modernization in most of our industries, both in equipment and in a willingness to realize that, under our form of civilization, we cannot be content merely with putting in new machinery. We have, as well, to do some concrete planning for the well-being of human beings who will, slowly but inexorably, be displaced by much of this new machinery.

It is part of our trouble, I think, that as our economy advanced by leaps and bounds it far outstripped the rest of the world. Up to now we have had no really serious competition to face. So we concluded that our know-how and our improved machinery would be able to meet the challenge of low-paid workers in many parts of the world whose standard of living was far below ours.

But the time has come when we must take a much more comprehensive view of the whole world economic situation. The time has come for planning on a long-range scale. It is the world of tomorrow for which we must prepare or we are going to find ourselves at the end of the procession.

Our old economic theories are not going to prove a successful guide to the future. We are becoming dimly aware of that even now. We must think and plan on a broader scale than ever before, on a scale that goes beyond our own borders, a scale that encompasses the world.

The needs of the world are infinite. If we are going to prove that our form of economy is able to meet those needs; even, indeed, if we are to keep abreast of the rate of advancement of other—and, as we thought, less fortunate, less efficient—nations, we must take a new look at our economic revolution.

Again we can learn by the lessons of past history. For instance, if Great Britain, instead of muddling through, had stopped to analyze the long-range effects of its first industrial revolution, 150 years ago, the world of today would be an altogether different place. It was because no one tried to solve the problem of the workers displaced by machinery that the resulting misery and starvation of thousands upon thousands of people led Karl Marx to the erroneous conclusion that war was inevitable between industry and labor, that only through class warfare would the workers of the world be able to get their fair share of the good things of life.

Now the irony of this situation, the fact—one of the facts—which the Soviets so carefully shield from their people in the course of rewriting history in their own image, is that Karl Marx's conclusions were wrong. He, too, misread the future. In the course of painful adjustments over the years the British worker was able to acquire a larger and larger share of the good things of his world and, with it, to acquire more and more independence. And without violent revolution. Anyone who can compare the present living conditions of the British workers with those of the Soviet workers will find the evidence clear.

In his book *Russia, America, and the World* Louis Fischer said:

> Great Britain has, since the Second World War, granted freedom to India, Pakistan, Burma, Ceylon and Malaya in Asia and to several of her African possessions. Nevertheless, she was able, in the 13 years after that costly conflict, to build 3,000,000 family homes and introduce free medicine for all. This is not the capitalism Marx and Lenin knew when they lived in London.

The fact remains that, with foresight, with imagination, with courage to face the facts and analyze them, *and adapt to changes*, the British leaders of that first Industrial Revolution might have prevented the enslavement of millions of human beings in Communist countries and the world today might be a safer place in which to live.

One other fact has become increasingly evident. That is the ability of Western Europe, devastated, depleted, ruined at the end of World War II, to develop more rapidly than the United States. The reason for this, I think, is that the countries of Europe were stricken so deeply that they had to face the new situation more quickly than we did, and were forced to do something about it.

Not long ago, a bewildered foreign diplomat asked me to explain why Europe seems to have modernized its industry on a larger scale than we have and is therefore going ahead faster. Certainly today the countries of Western Europe in the Common Market group are more prosperous than ever before in their history.

The answer is fairly simple. With the inception of the Marshall Plan, which was designed to help Europe get back on its feet after the Second World War so that it would not become a financial drag on the United States, our best minds focused on the basic problems and helped European industrialists to retool their plants and to become as efficient as possible.

To quote Louis Fischer again:

> ... economists predicted that it would be a generation before Europe could crawl out from under the debris of the worst holocaust in the history of man.
>
> Europe's recovery has exceeded all expectations.... Europe this side of the Soviet bloc is the most prosperous area of its size and population on the earth. Nineteen countries, counting approximately 400,000,000 inhabitants, produce more and consume more than Russia plus her satellites, and have richer trained manpower resources and potentially bigger military power than the Soviet Union.

This is what comes of long-range planning!

During the depression, my husband was able to rally the forces of the nation because the cataclysm was so violent, so immediate, that everyone was forced to recognize the situation. But today, cushioned in prosperity, we have put off the moment for decision. The Swedish economist and sociologist Dr. Gunnar Myrdal has referred to the current stagnation of the United States economy as posing a danger to the entire non-Communist world. Why, he demanded, have American businessmen failed to do what every European country does—make an analytical forecast of what a greater growth rate for five or ten years implies?

Must we, again, be America the Unready?

It is true that, time and time again in our economic life, we have had to face changes brought about by new markets, new machinery, new conditions, but so far we have always been able to meet these changes without making any plans in advance. True, this has brought about a certain amount of dislocation, and to some people real hardship, but the economy as a whole has been strong enough to absorb the difficulty created by inadequate planning and preparation.

True, there have been times when industry has, in its own interests, held back new scientific discoveries or new machinery until it felt that those already in use had been paid for or had produced the amount of profit desired. This is why some people have said that it often took war conditions to bring to the fore advancements that were, in many cases, beneficial to all human beings.

But now it is essential that instead of hanging back we move forward.

Primary in its effect upon the American worker is the huge problem of automation. Automation has forced upon us totally new conditions that can no longer be ignored if we are to keep our economy strong and our labor force at work.

Vital in coping with the effects of automation and in meeting the inexhaustible needs of the world today is full production and full employment. For many years, American business has shied away from the philosophy of full production. Steel, for instance, which is basic in our general economy, has never in peacetime produced to its maximum capacity.

We all know the effects of underproduction—and underemployment. For a few organizations there are higher prices; for an increasing number of employable persons there is no income at all. This is a situation which we simply cannot afford to put aside any longer, hoping vaguely that it will take care of itself. It won't. With increasing automation there are fewer and fewer jobs of the familiar kind for our labor force.

This is happening now—today. It is happening not only to

the man who works with his hands but to the white-collar worker. In office after office, throughout this country, employee after employee is being eliminated and his desk remains empty. And there is no place else for him to go.

One thing we must all have learned by the bitter lessons of the past. Poverty is an expensive luxury. We cannot afford it.

It is high time for industry to accept the philosophy of full production, to realize that, in the light of the modern industrial revolution, new thinking must be done if we are to cope with a new condition.

It is not, of course, the well-being of our labor force alone that is at stake here. By supine lethargy we stand to lose much of the world market. While our production has been lagging, the Soviets are steadily increasing their output of steel and threatening that in twenty years they will have reached astronomical quantities.

What will happen when they achieve maximum production? They are already reaching markets all over the world where the needs are the greatest. There is an almost unlimited need for things in the areas of Asia and Africa that the Soviet Union can easily reach.

It seems only yesterday that the United States was regarded as the unchallenged example of economic progress in the world. But for the past ten years this has ceased to be true. In 1958, Mr. Allen W. Dulles was quoted in the *New York Times* as saying: "Whereas Soviet gross national product was about 35% of the United States in 1950 . . . by 1962 it may be about 50% of our own. This means that the Soviet economy has been growing and is expected to grow through 1962 at a rate roughly twice that of the economy of the United States."

Why is it that our industrial leaders have not come up with workable suggestions for meeting this challenge and for spurring our economy so that we may keep our position as the world's greatest producer? What, in short, are they afraid of?

Not long ago, I was speaking at a dinner of the Hudson Valley Chapter of Industrial Engineers. I talked with a young engineer who sat beside me.

"If you had told your company ten years ago," I said to him, "about what was likely to happen in the next few years, wouldn't we be far better prepared today?"

"Of course," he agreed, "but no one would listen."

The exasperating thing is that far too few people are listening now. Too few people are making use of the evidence of their own eyes, are taking into account the implications of the changes they see around them. Such planning as is done appears to be a series of stop-gap measures: a new housing development to relieve congestion; historic old houses and older trees torn down to make a parking lot for a shopping center, which, within a few years, will be inadequate to the demands made on it; an extra wing or room added to an overcrowded school; a substitute teacher to "fill in."

There appears to be a sad lack of long-range, far-sighted, intelligent planning to provide for conditions as they will exist not next month but next year and in the years to come.

In almost every community in the United States we can see the disappearance of old businesses and the appearance of new ones. Take New England, for instance. If you drive around Boston you will realize that while, at one time, the textile mills were the backbone of industry, today it is electronics that prevents Boston and its vicinity from becoming a depressed area.

But this seems to have led to no attempt whatsoever to train workers for new fields, no wide analysis of our working force and of the areas where preparation is needed to meet new and changing needs. Certainly our recurring and increasing unemployment problem, which lies at the very heart of our economy, can be solved only by a recognition of new conditions, by a wide program for the teaching of new skills.

The needs of labor and the needs of the world will not be met by the panacea of shorter hours and higher wages. They will be met by modernizing the skills of our labor force so that they will be equipped for the new kinds of work required in a new world.

"What was good enough for my parents is good enough for me," people still say. But it won't be good enough for their children. Their world will not be the one in which you have lived. Every age is an unknown country.

I am not saying that the solution of the unemployment problem, brought about by automation and the need for new skills, is simple. It seems to me almost inevitable that industry, labor, and government will have to cooperate in a massive retraining program; that our whole system of education will have to be upgraded because the new scientific developments in our economy are going to require better-educated people than we are now providing.

Even after the heartbreaking lesson of the depression of 1929, this country has been so far unwilling to face the fact that the heaviest burden any people can carry is unemployment. Why cannot we use the same productive kind of planning here that was used, with such striking success, by the Marshall Plan in Western Europe?

Let us look again at France and West Germany, which suffered such massive destruction during the Second World War. Because of the Marshall Plan and long-range economic planning, Germany has, with our help, made a spectacular comeback, and has been able to absorb into the ranks of its employed thousands upon thousands of refugees who, month after month, have arrived from behind the Iron Curtain. Today, France is absorbing refugees from Algeria into its economy and looks upon them as a real benefit.

None of this happened by chance or by drifting. It was based on conscious economic theory. If you have no unemployment you have no drag on your economy.

When we look beyond our own noses at the world situation we see that we are not in this economic revolution alone. It is worldwide and it should, in the nature of things, be easier for Americans to cope with it than for the millions who are starting the long, slow, painful climb into civilization.

In 1955, it was estimated that 59 percent of American families or unattached individuals had an annual income, before income tax, of more than $4,000. The per capita incomes of other so-called "wealthy nations" were then roughly fixed at about $500 a year. But 80 percent of the world lives far below that level. In India, for instance, per capita income is only $60 a year, a figure that, judging by the tragic estimates of malnutrition, does not even meet basic animal needs.

If we look back to the hundred years, more or less, that were required in the West between the onset of the first Industrial Revolution and the time when people in general began to benefit by it, we may have some faint conception of what lies ahead of the poor nations of the world, which are, without any preparation, meeting the industrial revolution head on, without training, without equipment. At their present rate of per capita income growth—slightly over 1 percent a year—they may in the next half century, if their populations do not continue to increase at a geometric rate, reach a per capita income of about $200 a year, which is still far below that of the most impoverished of European peasants.

Once, however, the benefits of an economic revolution can be understood, once the first signs of improvement are discerned, there can be no turning back. After man discovered the benefit of a house he did not revert to a cave. So the struggle will go on.

But as these millions in underdeveloped countries start their slow, agonizing advance, they are bound to look about them for guideposts, if not for help. The people of Africa, for instance, see that India is improving her economy year by year, but at a slow rate. They believe, on the other hand, that the people of Red China are developing faster. What is this going to mean to them? True, they learn that this development is made at the price of human freedom, but the first freedom of man, I contend, is the freedom to eat. When the choice is as clear-cut as that, how many people will sell—and gladly— their hope of freedom for the certainty of bread?

If that is the only choice we leave them, who is to cast the first stone? Certainly I cannot. I have seen too many small children playing along the banks of Indian rivers, their bellies swollen from starvation.

The future of our American way of life in the face of the determined Soviet thrust toward the uncommitted nations depends upon our ability to win them to our side. The results, if we should fail to do so, are evident even to the blind. With the uncommitted nations lined up on the Soviet side, with the loss of our world markets, we would find ourselves standing alone.

Does anyone really feel that, cut off from allies, from markets, from necessary products for our own industries, we could continue to flourish, that we could be anything but an isolated and impotent island in a Communist sea?

The answer then is to review our economy in the light of present conditions, to build a new philosophy of full production and full employment here at home, and to help the young and impoverished nations to gain a better economy, a better way of life; to help them eradicate their lifelong enemy, hunger; to prove to them that they can have sufficient food and still eventually achieve their basic dream of full freedom as human beings.

But if we are going to sell this new way of life to the impoverished peoples we must first believe in it ourselves. We must relearn the deep faith in our country and in its system, which seems to have grown apathetic. To do so, the basic requirement, it seems to me, is to insure our own people full opportunity to have a share in the prosperity of their own country. This means that we must tackle the problem of unemployment on a full-scale basis.

To me it seems evident that the answer is not, as some labor leaders believe, more pay and shorter hours of work. I repeat this because it seems to me a vital mistake. It is a mere stop-gap, a thumb in the dike; it is not a solution.

Implicit in our American system is the idea that every man has a right to work. This idea has now been given world application in the Universal Declaration of Human Rights. When we accepted it for the United States I made the statement that the United States took this clause to mean that every government has the obligation to try to create an economic climate in which all who want work can find work, and preferably work suited to their particular abilities. I added that no government has a right to let its people starve. Therefore, if there is any reason, beyond their control, why individuals or groups cannot find work, the government has an obligation to create work over a period of time until the economy again can absorb its total employable population.

The equipment is here; the power is here; the needs are everywhere. There is nothing to stop us but lack of business and labor leadership, lack of imagination—and fear.

Some years ago, a distinguished industrialist took part in a symposium at the Harvard School of Business. At that time, he implored the business leaders of the country to begin to lead. He pointed out that they had fought bitterly every advancement of the people as a whole on the ill-founded idea that it would ruin business. They had fought an end to child labor; they had fought the twelve-hour day, and later the eight-hour day. They had fought the unions. Wasn't it time, he asked, for them to come to grips with their contemporary civilization?

One of the basic elements in our whole way of life, one of the elements that, for two hundred years, has attracted the peoples of the world to our shores, is our belief that each individual has a right to a better life and to better working conditions and a larger share of the prosperity of his country because, by having them, *he can develop his maximum potentialities as a human being.*

This is the ultimate purpose of our way of life. The state is the servant of the people, existing for his protection and his benefit. To the Soviets, the individual is a servant of the state, serving its ends blindly, and profiting only to the extent that his service is useful to the state.

Anyone who believes that in every human being there is a spark of the divine, that he is not merely an animal, must believe that to enable him to develop his potentialities to the maximum is the highest purpose his government and his society can fulfill. I can remember my husband's angry retort when someone suggested that he let the depression run its course without interference. "People aren't cattle, you know."

For countless generations, it is true, people were slow to

recognize this concept. Even devout Christians were uncon-
cerned about the existence of a vast majority of the desperately
poor, who were born in squalor and died in squalor; whose
lives, to borrow Hobbes's phrase, were "nasty, brutish, and
short."

Only in the twentieth century, perhaps, has anyone asked
why people are poor. Only in the past half century has an earnest effort been made to tackle the problem of poverty and
eliminate it. Only today has it become a matter for every man's
conscience. And now—for poverty is like a giant infection
which contaminates everything—we know that unless we can
eradicate it by the use of all our new scientific and economic
materials, it can in time destroy us. To make our economic
revolution serve the ends of the other economic revolutions in
the world and to win the battle is the price for our own survival and the survival of a way of life we cherish.

The economic revolution, as I have said before, exists in one
form and another in practically every country of the world.
No economic planning, anywhere today, can be based exclusively on the welfare of a single area. There are, of course, the
disgruntled murmurs of a few people: "But I can't see *why* we
give money and food to those people. They don't even like us.
Why should we go out of our way to help them?"

There are people who still quote approvingly the words of
Warren G. Harding in 1920: "Stabilize America first, prosper
America first, exalt America first." We know what came of
that.

There is another, more belligerent comment: "Why should
we give assistance to any country whose form of government
differs from ours? Above all, why should we lift a hand for
people whose system of economy differs from ours?"

Here, I believe, is the area of thought that is going to require
more fresh thinking than any other. Up to now we have been
thinking a great many things that aren't so. So, in our thinking about such words as *democracy* and *capitalism*, in relation
to other countries of the world, including our allies, we often
find ourselves basing our judgments on the wrong premises.

The word *democracy* is loosely used. Today, England has a

socialist monarchy; so has Sweden; the government of France is dominated by one man. We continue, however, to call them democracies. Certainly we do not have the temerity or the impertinence to tell them that their governments, their economies must follow our pattern—or else.

In dealing with the new nations of the world we must relearn the meaning of that noble word *respect*. That is the only sound and enduring basis for any relationship among peoples, as it is among individuals. We must learn to respect the various methods of development of the new nations, so long as they grant to the individual certain basic rights. We cannot say to them: "If you will accept our way of life we will help you." If we are going to build a strong and peaceful world, we must be intelligent enough to help new nations in terms of their needs and not of our personal theories.

What will happen to the new nations; what, indeed, may happen to us, depends upon our capacity to think afresh, to understand the historical trends, and to plan in accordance with what is actually happening, not what we would prefer to have happening.

A respect for the rights of other peoples to determine their forms of government and their economy will not weaken our democracy. It will inevitably strengthen it. One of the first things we must get rid of is the idea that democracy is tantamount to capitalism. Not long ago, I saw a pamphlet prepared by an industrialist, in which he stated categorically that capitalism meant democracy.

The most fleeting glance at past history makes clear that this is not true. Capitalism flourished long before the concept of democracy existed. The two are not necessarily equated. There are many countries in the world for which our system is unworkable. There is no reason, however, why we cannot live and work with them in peace and without friction. Actually, our dealings with Norway and Sweden have never been ruffled because they operate on a socialist economy.

Long ago, in one of his speeches, my husband said, "This generation has a rendezvous with destiny." I think ours has, too. It hangs in the balance whether we will meet the challenge or whether we will drift; whether we will lead or whether we will follow; whether we will be flexible or whether we will be rigid.

Fresh thinking, long-range action, full production on all fronts instead of curtailing work and hours. It is not more vacation we need—it is more vocation.

A basic area in which we need new vision and long-range planning is agriculture. So far, and to the bewilderment—the deep-seated anger—of the starving of the world, our major planning has involved cutting down on the production of food-stuffs.

We have a quandary. While we worry about the production of too much food, one person out of four in the world goes to bed hungry every night of his life. It seems to me preposterous that our only way of meeting the problem is to cut down on food production. What we apparently have failed to grasp is that, in this new world in which we live, the collective hunger of great masses of people, wherever they may be, will affect our long-range welfare, just as though they were our own people.

Certainly it is high time that we rethink our whole foreign aid program to tie in with the immediate pressures of hunger in the world. From the most selfish standpoint of our own self-preservation, we might well change the course of future events by looking at the situations and problems with a broader vision and more imagination.

Today, we pay more for the storage of our surplus foods than for our entire economic aid to Asia. This strikes me as economic madness. If we were to distribute this food where it is most needed, on terms of long-range credits, we could feed the hungry, build good will, strengthen new nations, and—in the long run—profit financially. To do this will require careful and intelligent planning to avoid dislocation of the economics of other nations producing surplus food. But I believe such planning can be achieved.

Again, from the standpoint of long-range planning, we must face some unpalatable facts. Our high standard of living is not a gift from heaven; it is dependent upon a number of factors, including full employment, and the continuing development of foreign markets for our products. But, until we have helped raise the living standards of other peoples in the world to the point where they want, need, and can buy our products—and you can't do that to any people until they have been adequately fed—we will be unable to create new markets and inevitably, slowly or quickly, our own standard of living will begin to falter and decline.

But we should not, as we have done in the past, send grain that has spoiled from being stored too long. We should not send wheat and corn to people who don't eat them. This sort of thing does not make sense.

With our wide range of climate and soil, with some intelligent planning, we could, in this country, grow a variety of food products that would meet the needs of the world far more adequately and suitably than we do now. And here, as farming becomes more and more mechanized, the problem of growing new and varied crops is easier to solve.

Certainly, with agriculture as with industry, the dynamic leadership of the American people would be shown better not by curtailment but by full production.

There is one more area where long-range planning is basic to the future well-being of the American people. That is in the preservation of our natural resources. Here, year after year, and most vociferously during election years, we suffer from the selfish claims of a few people to exploit the natural resources of the country for their private profit, and without regard to the ultimate impoverishment of all the people. Our forests are cut down, our rivers and lakes are polluted. We have created dust bowls through short-sightedness, stupidity, and greed.

Those of us who have flown over vast areas of desert, such as you look down upon in Iran or Israel, have learned something about how men destroy the fertility of the world in which they live. It is essential that people learn the elementary facts about how to preserve the trees, the topsoil, and life-giving water.

Not so many years ago, some short-sighted farmers nearly succeeded in turning a large area of the United States into a desert. At that time the price of wheat was very high. In their eagerness to plant a few more acres, the farmers plowed up land in the dry, windy sections of the Great Plains which should have been kept as pasture.

In the early thirties this area was stricken by drought. The destruction of the land was so apparent and so disastrous that vigorous efforts were taken to stop it. Thousands of acres were converted back from wheat farming to grasslands. Contour plowing and the building of hundreds of small dams conserved the rainfall and helped restore enough vegetation to anchor down the topsoil. Long rows of trees—known as shelter belts—were planted on the northern and western sides of many farms, to break the force of the prevailing winds. Gradually the barren lands were restored; and when the next cycle of droughts came, some twenty years later, far less topsoil blew away. Little by little, the farmers of the Great Plains have learned to work with nature, instead of against it.

This reminds me of a trip made through the southwest desert, a bleak, empty, and frightening land. To my delight, our car finally reached a welcoming shade. There were flowers growing and fruits. There was the fresh sound of running water.

"But how did this happen in a desert?" I asked the man at that improbable little fruit stand in the cool shade.

"We planted trees," he said dryly.

5.

THE SOCIAL REVOLUTION

Be an opener of doors for such as come after thee, and do
not try to make the universe a blind alley.

RALPH WALDO EMERSON

The economic revolution is bringing with it social changes
that are being felt everywhere. As the life of human beings is
lifted above the animal level, they become aware of new aspirations, beyond the immediate and pressing need for food to
eat, and develop a passionate longing for independence. What
is stirring like yeast everywhere is the revolution of equality,
the assertion by men and women of their human dignity, and
their demand for its recognition and acceptance by others.

Certainly it is this particular revolution which the United
States should be able to win, hands down, because this is the
concept upon which our life is based.

"We know," Barbara Ward wrote recently, "that the passionate desire of men to see themselves as the equals of other
human beings without distinctions of class or sex or race or
nationhood is one of the driving forces of our day."

We know—yes. But what are we doing about it? We are
dealing today with millions upon millions of people of diverse
religions. That should be easy for us. This country, after all,
was founded upon the principle of religious freedom. But how
is it working out in actual practice?

Many of us still remember, with shame, the burning crosses,
the revival of the Ku Klux Klan that accompanied Al Smith's
campaign for the Presidency. All of us remember, more recently,

during John Kennedy's campaign, the fantastic claims that, if a Catholic were elected to the Presidency, the Pope would take over the direction of the policies of the nation. Even now when this nonsense has been shown to be without foundation, I know of no one who has withdrawn his original cry of alarm or admitted that he was mistaken.

In a very real sense, the United States is the world's show window of the democratic processes in action. We know, too well, what people see when they look in that window. They see Little Rock and Baton Rouge and New Orleans. They see Albany, Georgia. They see the deep-rooted prejudice, the stubborn ignorance of large groups of our citizens, which have led to injustice, inequality, and, sometimes, even brutality.

I think what most of us remember most vividly about the riots and the cruelty of Little Rock, Baton Rouge, and New Orleans is the pictures we saw in our newspapers, pictures which gave us a tremendous shock when we realized what ugliness and degradation mass fear could bring out in human beings.

Grown women wanted to kill one poor little nine-year-old girl, one of the children going into the Little Rock school. The cold fact is hard to believe that anywhere in our country women would be screaming for the death of a child because she was going into a white school. Yet this is what happened. This was the result of mass fear and mass psychology.

The beast in us is something we have to learn to control. It would be wise if we came to realize how it functions on many different levels. Habit is one of the controlling factors. If we can learn to subdue the emotions arising from prejudice, if we can learn that the social revolution in which we are engaged should, among other things, provide all our people with an equal opportunity to enjoy the benefits that have been the privileges of a few, we are going to be astonished to discover that many whom we considered incapable of development were only underprivileged; that given the opportunity for education there are latent endowments which will be valuable not only to these people in themselves but to their country and the world as well.

It is this minority of strident and prejudiced people, with

their unwillingness to accept race equality—at whatever cost—who provide the Communists with most of their ammunition against the democratic system, who are loudest in their expression of hatred for Communism.

One of the most difficult experiences I have ever been through was that of serving as Chairman for the Commission of Inquiry into the Administration of Justice in the Freedom Struggle, held in Washington in May of 1962. I found it difficult—and intolerably painful—to accept the fact that things such as I have described could happen here in these United States. This was the kind of thing the Nazis had done to the Jews of Germany—and there, also, as a misguided effort to demonstrate their race superiority.

Only by focusing the attention of the nation as a whole upon this situation can we find a remedy for it. The overwhelming pressure of public opinion would accomplish more than any other single factor to rectify the condition and to help eliminate it.

What emerged, of course, was that, as had been true since before the Civil War, it was largely whites whose economic condition was little better than that of the Negroes who represented the most virulent element, concentrating the chief hatred, prejudice, and—yes, downright brutality. It was, perhaps, the only way in which they could proclaim their superiority. They appeared to be terrified for fear the Negroes would be permitted to stand on their own merits, and might, in many cases, leave them far behind.

And here, too, emerged another and unmistakable similarity to the Nazism we had believed destroyed—at least in Germany. Most of the dictators of the West—Franco, Mussolini, Hitler—claimed that they were "saving" their lands from the threat of Communism. Today, as I have learned over and over to my cost, one needs only to be outspoken about the unfair treatment of the Negro to be labeled "Communist." I had regarded such expression to be the only honorable and civilized course for a citizen of the United States.

To digress for a moment, this recurring matter of labeling

"Communist" anyone who does not agree with you is essentially an act of dishonesty and it should be nailed every time for what it is. Few of the Southern politicians who resented my stand on integration ever troubled to examine it: Instead they said "Communist." The Nazis excelled at this sort of thing. It has no place in America.

To return to the Commission of Inquiry, there appeared before us a succession of people who had set out to test the operation of the laws in regard to civil rights. The methods they used were peaceful enough. Some of them indulged in public prayer; some of them rode on buses to see whether segregation was still practiced on buses and in terminal facilities; some of them sat in at lunch counters for the same purposes; some of them picketed a segregated lunchroom for *one minute and a half*! And one young man was teaching Negroes, who had been driven from their farms for attempting to register to vote, how to make a kind of leather tote bag so that they could earn enough money to hold back starvation.

These were the people who suffered indignity, danger, arrest on preposterous charges; people who are even now facing incredibly long prison sentences; people who, in some cases, were treated with a brutality that sickens one to think of.

I would like to quote from the words of Carl Rachlin, one of the counsels for the Commission, who opened that horrifying hearing, because it seems to me vital that these facts should be clearly known to all the American people:

> . . . patterns of official conduct interfering with the rights of Negroes to pursue activities in every way lawful . . .
>
> Mass arrests and jailing on criminal charge upon criminal charge, some dreadfully serious, is the pattern in Baton Rouge. . . .
>
> In Mississippi, it is impossible to obtain a bail bond for any arrest in a civil rights case. As a result cash bail has had to be raised in these cases in that state. . . .
>
> Much of the testimony will show brutality, official indignity and failure of police protection. At the same time it will show,

we believe, the good faith, the good spirits, the peaceful intentions of the people who participated in such activities in behalf
of equality. . . .

The normal appeal of American citizens to petition their state
government and representatives for redress of wrongs is . . .
closed to the participants in these activities.

I'd like to look for a moment at a few of these cases, at conditions that could only have existed because, as a people, we
are paying only lip service to our democratic principles; we
have, at least in this area, been tending to lose our social
revolution.

Ronnie Moore was one of those who sat in at a lunch coun-
ter; one of those who participated in the picketing which lasted
just one minute and a half. He was arrested and had to raise a
cash bond of $1,500. Rearrested, the charge became "conspir-
acy to commit criminal mischief." There was an additional
$2,000 bond. After serving twenty-one days in jail, he was
released, and this time arrested for "criminal trespassing and
disturbing the peace." (He was taking shelter from the rain.)
By now the bond was up to $6,500.

For fifty-eight days, Ronnie and another young man were
kept in a seven-by-seven-foot cell, without a window; and
taken out only twice a week for a shower. After his release
there was a new charge, "criminal anarchy," and the bond had
now reached a total of $16,500.

Let's take another case, that of a young Negro minister with
a group of students who intended to pray and sing in protesting the arrest of the picketers. They sustained a barrage of
forty-seven tear gas bombs; police dogs attacked them. Later,
three hundred young students had to be treated for dog bites
and tear gas, and for having been trampled upon.

A white boy named John Robert Zellner, the young son of a
Methodist minister in south Alabama, was arrested for protesting the expulsion of a colored girl from a high school. The
charge, ironically enough, was "disturbing the peace and contributing to the delinquency of a minor."

While he was a prisoner in the white section of the jail, the other white prisoners, furious because he was attempting to help Negroes, "threatened me with castration . . . said if I went to sleep I'd wake up with a knife in my back."

"I thought," Robert commented during his testimony, "it was quite ironic that the United States was able to launch a man into space and let him go around the world three times and yet they weren't able to take care of a small human relations problem."

Frank Nelson, another white man, who had been a student in engineering at Cooper Union and then served with the United States Coast Guard as a civil engineer, was asked: "Why are you, as a white person, participating in these activities?"

"Actually," he answered, "it was just a matter of getting down to finally doing what just about everybody thinks is correct and I . . . got tired of sitting around in the living room and discussing how bad things were . . . and finally decided to see if I could perhaps do something to change things."

How much must be changed was made clear in the repeated pictures of brutality: of policemen directing some of the vandalism, of the police dogs and the tear gas, of the young man who was blackjacked and had to have fifty-seven stitches taken in his head; of the white boy on whose hand they put what they called a "wrist breaker," a metal clamp which they tightened until the victim fainted several times from pain.

Then—unspeakable ugliness in this our own country—"An electric stock probe, used in stockyards to stock cattle and make them move along, was used around the private parts. It was very painful stuff. I was picked up and held in the air by the private parts." This was the young man who had attempted peacefully to teach the dispossessed Negroes to earn a living by making tote bags.

It was because of such people as this that Gerald Johnson, a Negro student, answered as he did when he was asked, "What made you get in all this trouble?"

"I have grown up under segregationist rule . . . and I didn't like the way things worked. . . . When I heard people like Bob

Zellner . . . the things that they have been through for people like me . . . I couldn't face sitting back doing nothing, and I don't want my children to grow up under something like that."

"In other words," he was asked, "you wanted to fight on the home front for some of the liberties and privileges of American citizenship that the Negro soldiers fought overseas to guarantee to the rest of the world?"

"Right," he said.

When I first introduced this painful and shameful subject, I said that its solution rests with public opinion. So it does. The President of the United States can lead only if he has followers. It is the voice of America that he must hear clearly.

Realizing at the inquiry that many of the young victims of race prejudice and savagery were bitter about the kind of judges before whom their cases were heard, I tried to make the following point:

> I think you have to realize that under our political system, judges have to be endorsed by the senators and congressmen of their district.
>
> Now, unless you can awaken public opinion to have some effect in the South, you are asking the President to risk very often a vote on his Administration's policy bills and perhaps not get them passed because he has refused to follow recommendations of the elected representatives of the district.
>
> This points up, I think, the need for the individual citizen to be awakened and held responsible, because it is the people in these areas who are really responsible.
>
> They elect their representatives. They are the ones who feel this way and I think they will respond to the real feeling of the rest of the country, if it is brought out and crystallized and made clear what they are doing to their country in the eyes of the world and in the eyes of their own nation and of their own people.

The great Russian pianist Anton Rubinstein once said hotly, "Despots never think the people ripe enough for freedom." We still have too many people in this country who feel that the

Negro is not ripe for equality, in education, in the economy, in housing, in opportunity.

If this is our lesson to the nations who are trying to bridge the gap between primitive living and the age of nuclear fission, and to those other nations whose culture was already old while ours was primitive, they can only reject it entirely. In making their great transition to the modern world, these people need all the help we can give them; they need our respect; they need our recognition of their essential dignity as human beings. But while we fail in such recognition to those of our own people whose skins are colored—as are the skins of two out of three of all the peoples of the world—they will never believe in our sincerity, never believe that we pay more than lip service to the ideals of democracy which we claim to defend.

One of our blind spots comes with the persistent and fondly cherished idea that, because some peoples have lagged behind in civilization and in cultural development, they are congenitally incapable of that development. This has been disproved over and over by such anthropologists as Margaret Mead. It can be disproved almost daily if we look about at some of the magnificent achievements of Negroes.

"You can't," say the people who take comfort in speaking in clichés, "change human nature."

Now the only way we can judge human nature is by human behavior, and behavior is modified and changed and developed and transformed by training and surroundings, by social customs and economic pressures. When we wince, sickened, at some of the grosser violence of an Elizabethan play, we are simply indicating that our "human nature" has undergone some drastic alterations in the past three hundred years.

Some years ago, I studied a snapshot which I have never forgotten. It was a picture showing two men standing outside a primitive grass hut in the Philippines. One of the men was naked except for a loincloth. He had wild bushy hair. In either hand he held a skull. He was a headhunter from the bush.

The young man beside him wore a white suit and glasses. In his hand he carried a small professional bag. He was a trained physician, working in the field of public health. He was the headhunter's son!

That transition, from headhunter to scientist, was not even the work of one generation; it was the work of perhaps fifteen years at the outside. What had been required to "change human nature" and make the leap from the Stone Age to the present? Opportunity, education, recognition of his human potentialities, and a chance to be trained for a job in the field for which he was best suited.

But we must not overlook the operative factor. The young scientist had been trained. Too often, we tend to expect too much of people to whom we have given no training.

As far back as I can remember every attempt at improvement in the standard of living for Negroes was met by complaints that they were not ripe for equality. Because I was interested in housing, I was involved many years ago in one of the first slum clearance projects. People said, "It is ridiculous to give a bathroom to these people. They don't know how to use it. Some of them are keeping coal in the bathtub."

Our answer to that was to put a director in charge who helped people to learn about their new surroundings and to adapt to them. As soon as they became familiar with the various conveniences they used them properly.

Of course, difficulties are apt to develop if people are provided with modern conveniences without being given any guidance or instruction in their use. Certainly it is unfair to expect people without training to use properly what they have never encountered before.

And here, I think, there is a responsibility both for the whites and the Negroes. Too often, it is true, Negroes from underprivileged areas move into apartments or neighborhoods and, because they have been taught no better, clutter the hallways with filth and arouse reasonable resentment and alarm in the white tenants, who naturally do not want to see their way of life deteriorate. The function of democratic living is not to lower standards but to raise those that have been too low.

It seems to me that men like Martin Luther King might well perform a great service to the cause of equality for which they fight so gallantly, if they were to help some of the under-privileged Negroes to prepare themselves to fit in to better surroundings.

If we are going to belong to our world we must take into account the fact that the majority of the peoples of the world are non-whites. We must learn to surmount this deep-seated prejudice about color. Certainly we must face the evidence that the color of the skin does not regulate the superiority or inferiority of the individual.

Now and then, when I have pointed out example after example of non-whites whose superiority in their fields cannot be challenged, I am told, "Oh, but those are exceptions." The same thing may be said of superior people among the white population. They, too, are exceptions. Most of us fall far below them in ability and in achievement.

It is interesting to study our own racial problems and to compare them with the problems that exist in Africa. The basic issues are quite different. I have had African nationals tell me that the struggle for the liberation of the Africans from colonial powers was initiated by the efforts of the Africans themselves. Here in America, they said, it has nearly always been the whites and not the Negroes who saw the injustices and tried to correct them. Indeed, it is the success of the Africans in attaining their liberty, and the dignity that has grown out of their new status, that has lent a new spirit to our own Negroes.

Of course, one of the stumbling blocks in creating this equality in our own social revolution is another cliché like the one "You can't change human nature." This is used as a final stopper to any discussion of the subject. "Would you," these people ask, "like to see your daughter marry a Negro?"

Now this is a red herring if I ever saw one. Racial intermarriage is not involved in job equality, in educational equality, in housing equality. In fact, I strenuously doubt that any father who ever asked that challenging question had the slightest fear that his daughter wanted to marry a Negro. None the less, the inference from his question is that his daughter is quite likely to do so unless she is prevented by the enforced segregation of Negroes.

All this is really preposterous. No one knows it as well as the person who clings to his question as though it were actually an answer to the problem. The immense majority of people instinctively seek their own kind. France, for instance, has long had race equality but comparatively little intermarriage has resulted. The issue of intermarriage is used as a stumbling block in the path of human justice; it is used to hold back opportunity for millions of our citizens to develop their full potentialities in an ambience of mutual respect.

True, there are occasional—but very rare—cases of great attraction between different races. There are some successful marriages; for instance, those of Walter White with a white woman and Marian Anderson with a white man. And I know of others. But these, of course, are exceptional people, strong enough to escape the aura of martyrdom that so often hamstrings such a marriage.

But I still contend that the use of this fatuous question to prevent the development of the Negro race is essentially an act of dishonesty. It is used, like sleight of hand, to distract our attention from inequalities in wages, in living quarters, in education, that are an ineffaceable disgrace to us as a people.

It often seems to me that prejudice so blinds us that we see only what we expect to see, what we want to see. An example of this comes to mind.

At Wiltwick, a school for problem children across the river from Hyde Park, a school in which I have long had a deep interest, there was a small boy named Tommy. One weekend he was allowed to go home to visit his mother. When he returned, he went to see his social worker, a gentle and understanding woman.

"I hates white people," he told her.

"Oh, no, Tommy!"

"Yes, I does. They makes my Mommy cry. They're mean to her."

"I don't blame you for not liking the ones who are mean to your mother, but not *all* white people, Tommy!"

"Yes, I does!"

"Do you hate me?"

"Oh, no, I loves you."

"But I'm white." In fact, she was a Norwegian with blond hair, big blue eyes, and a milky complexion.

"You is?" He looked at her in surprise. Then he patted her cheek consolingly. "You sure don't look it."

While it is essential for us to cope at once with the social revolution in this country we must, at the same time, learn to adjust to the social revolutions in other parts of the world. This is not only a matter of common decency, it is a matter of common sense. If there were no desire on the part of the African peoples to enter the modern world we would not be able to develop new markets for ourselves.

These people are looking for guidance on that long and difficult climb, a climb that they must make swiftly. We took our guidance in building a nation from the patterns of England and Western Europe, using what we needed, what served our purpose; developing new lines where we felt them to be an improvement.

Where are the Africans to turn for guidance? To the Eastern world or to the Western world? One thing is sure. We cannot convince them of the value of our ideas, our principles, and our ideals unless we know clearly what they are, unless we are able to express them, unless we are prepared to implement them. And we cannot address any people successfully unless we know and understand—and respect—that people.

We can no longer oversimplify. We can no longer build lazy and false stereotypes: Americans are like this, Russians are like that, a Jew behaves in such a way, a Negro thinks in a different way. The lazy generalities—"You know how women are. . . . Isn't that just like a man?"

The world cannot be understood from a single point of view.

If we cannot understand the people who make up our own country, how are we going to understand the people we are trying to lead in the world as a whole? The Soviets tell them that they are better suited to be of assistance to them because they are closer to their problems than we are. Our simple assertion that this is not true is meaningless. We must prove that it is not true.

How? Well, the Soviets invite people to their country and show them what they want them to see. But our country is open to all who wish to move around. They can judge for themselves. Both the good and the bad are open for inspection.

And, on the whole, even our bad spots are not as bad as most visitors have been led to believe. Often the reality of a situation will seem much better than the fantastic tales that have grown up about what actually goes on in our country. For instance, a few years ago, the idea of most Africans about what happened to the colored people in this country was so completely erroneous and exaggerated that the stories were unrecognizable. Whatever visitors from these countries saw here was a vast improvement on what they had been told. None the less, our obligation to improve our own conditions is not diminished.

One thing is certain: in this modern world of ours we cannot afford to forget that what we do at home is important in relation to the rest of the world. The sooner we learn this, the sooner we will understand the meaning of our social revolution.

It is not too much to say that our adjustment to our own social revolution will affect almost every country in the world. Nor is it too much to say that we should be able to make our adjustment with comparative ease. What is required of us is infinitesimal compared to the adjustments that are to be made in the backward nations—in prejudice, in superstition, in ignorance, in habits and customs. They are coming out of the bush; we have only to come out of the darkness of our own blind prejudice and fear into the steady light of reason and humanity.

You will tell me, perhaps, that to cope successfully with our social revolution we must bring about a revolution in the mentality of the American people. While there is much truth in this, it is well to remember that, in many respects and in many

areas of the United States, that revolution has been fought—
and won. In his first inaugural my husband said, "We do not
distrust the future of essential democracy."

The ensuing years, up to the Second World War, revealed
that, when they had taken a wrong turning, the American
people were willing to shift their position, to look freshly at
conditions, and to find new methods of tackling them. And
they were able to do this within the framework of the American system; they were able to find a middle course that upheld
the capitalistic system at a time when most of the world seemed
to have adopted the policy of extremes—either the extreme
right of Nazism or the extreme left of Communism.

What we have failed too often to do is to appeal to this
capacity for flexibility in the people.

The revolution in our social thinking appears, in capsule
form, to my eyes, in one family I know well—my own. My
mother-in-law belonged to the established world of the last
century. She accepted its shibboleths without questioning. To
her these things were true.

When she died, in September, 1941, my husband felt strongly
this ending of an unshakable world behind him. And yet, he
told me, it was probably as well for his mother to leave us at
that time. She was immersed in her old world and the new one
was alien to her. The adjustment for her would have been
impossible.

In using the term, I do not mean adjustment merely to the
dramatic and obvious physical changes: to modern transportation and electrical gadgets and all the scientific inventions that
have transformed our world. Within an incredibly short time,
no matter how drastic is such change, one adjusts to it. It simply becomes one more convenience.

No, the basic change in the social revolution has been the
change in values. To my mother-in-law, for instance, there
were certain obligations that she, as a privileged person, must
fulfill. She fed the poor, assisted them with money, helped
them with medical expenses. This was a form of charity
required of her.

The point of view that she simply could not accept was my

husband's. He believed—as I trust most civilized people believe now—that human beings have rights as human beings: a right to a job, a right to education, a right to health protection, a right to human dignity, a right to a chance of fulfillment.

This is the inevitable growth in our thinking as a nation— the practical application of democratic principles. No one today would dare refer to the mass of the people, as Alexander Hamilton once did, as "that great beast." And that, perhaps, is a minor victory in the long battle for human rights.

6.

THE REVOLUTION IN EDUCATION

... our training must prepare individuals to face a novelty of conditions. But there can be no preparation for the unknown. ... We require such an understanding of the present conditions as may give us some grasp of the novelty which is about to produce a measurable influence on the immediate future.

ALFRED NORTH WHITEHEAD

If we are to cope successfully with our revolutions in science, in the economy, in social areas, we must prepare for the revolution in education that will be required to meet, to understand, and to master the new conditions. Without a totally new approach to education our young people are not going to be equipped to cope with the world of the future.

It is not too much to say that our whole attitude toward education must be changed. The training of the past—too long inadequate even for the purposes of the past—will not serve in preparing the youngsters of today to meet new conditions; above all, conditions which none of us can clearly foresee. It is one thing to provide a simple skill that can be applied to a given situation. It is quite another thing—and a new, a revolutionary thing—to prepare young people to meet an unknown world, to solve unforeseeable problems, and to adapt their skills, their intelligence, and their knowledge to new situations that are developing with lightning speed.

In other words, it should be our objective to train minds as tools that can be used for a lifetime, inquiring minds, curious minds, seeking, constantly refueling their ideas and their information. Certainly, this means a new concept of education to fit the young for the small new world in which they are going to play the leading part in the future. Or, if we continue as we are going in education, they may play no part at all.

Have we been honest and brave enough to make clear to our young people that we could not, if we would, provide the specific education that would equip them for the coming world, whose face no one knows? Have we told them bluntly that the best we can do is to give them skills, to train the mind so that it becomes a flexible tool, to provide techniques for learning and for finding information, to provide the ability to apply such information as they have to the acquiring of more information, that will work to solve new problems? Above all, have we attempted to give our own minds the flexibility to accept change and to welcome rather than fear it?

Undoubtedly, one of the most vital elements in preparing the young to meet and cope with questions that cannot now be foreseen is this: unless people are willing to face the unfamiliar they cannot be creative in any sense, for creativity always means the doing of the unfamiliar, the breaking of new ground. It is from this creative element, which we should be stimulating now, that all the new ideas of the future will come.

It is this creative element, too, which, when activated, can afford perhaps the keenest satisfaction a human being can experience. Often, I think, our young people have not been trained to see where the real satisfactions of life are to be found. In school we find ways of learning without much effort; we stress play and having fun. There are, I have heard, some two to three hundred thousand teachers in the United States who are teaching "frill and fun subjects."

Children rush from school to basketball games or television programs. At the age of the keenest curiosity and the widest interest, they are, it seems to me, missing the boat altogether. Anyone who has watched small children at play will observe that, for the most part, the play is earnest. They are happiest when it is creative. They want to accomplish something, to make something. But when they are permitted, even encouraged, to accomplish as little as possible, this early innate impulse begins to fade.

This is, in part, a result of the kind of values which our children are being taught. I find that, too often, in telling our young of the blessings and advantages of our system of life, we stress heavily our materialistic advantages. We treat them as ends in themselves rather than as means to a better life.

Too often, in their homes, children hear great stress put on possessions, as though they were goals and not merely appurtenances. This produces a value concept built on outward achievements, on the purely materialistic, that has done our country so much harm in the eyes of the world, and that tends to stimulate in the child a desire to acquire these material possessions, these tokens of "success," rather than to strive for a more abiding and more deeply satisfying value.

With all the furor, with all the thousands of books on educational theory and philosophy and methods, with all the tedious complaints about the inadequacy of our educational system as it exists today, we are doing almost nothing to rectify the situation. Rates of teachers' pay remain too low to attract the best teachers unless they are so dedicated that they are willing to make a sacrifice we have no right to ask of them.

At a time when, like it or not, one's status in this country is predicated to a large degree on the amount of his income, we are being peculiarly short-sighted in underpaying the purveyors of education.

One of the results of this policy is that industry has to spend vast sums to take up the slack in training employees for their jobs. At the same time it is losing the benefits that would accrue by having trained minds capable of sparking new ideas. Another loss occurs to the country as a whole. The high-school graduate, on an average, earns during his lifetime $150,000 more than the grade-school graduate; the college graduate $150,000 more than the high-school graduate.

Compare the money spent in this country on education with

that spent on alcohol, on tobacco, on cosmetics. Congress is willing to allot huge sums for vague purposes of whose ultimate success they have no assurance, but not for education, whose incontestable benefits we know well. There is little federal money forthcoming for school buildings in which children will have adequate and comfortable and safe surroundings. Apparently Congress would rather build air-raid shelters under the schools than improve the buildings themselves, although, according to the latest information I have received from Washington, there is no plan for what happens when they eventually come out from the shelters. This kind of psychology is one of defeat, which evades all the main issues and does nothing to prepare young people to cope any better with conditions than their fathers have done.

Now and then, we hear the ominous phrase, "Education for survival." This seems to me a hideous concept. This is placing the bogeyman of fear at the forefront of our objectives. It is not fear, it is freedom we must maintain.

Never have we needed as acutely as now, in a world in ferment, shifting and changing its course, often without direction, the full use of all the brain power we have. It is from the improved training of minds that most of the advances of the past century have come. We need every single mind. We cannot afford to have any potential talent or ability dulled to apathy by unimaginative teaching, by a lack of training in specific skills, by a failure to use the mind as a tool for finding more information.

From the beginning, the American people as a whole have believed that investment in people is the soundest and most long-reaching investment that we can make. The more complicated the type of government—and Jefferson pointed out long ago that democracy is the most complicated—the more education is needed.

But here, too, we have had a tendency to overestimate the amount of compulsory schooling which has been provided by the United States. Here, too, we have been inclined to believe things that weren't so. Actually, it was not until 1852 that the first compulsory school law was passed in Massachusetts, requiring only twelve weeks of school, and applying only to children from eight to fourteen. It was not until 1920 that the last compulsory school law was passed, in Mississippi.

Recently, Ambassador Galbraith, speaking to an audience in India, said: "A dollar, or a rupee, invested in the intellectual improvement of human beings will regularly bring a greater increase in national income than a dollar or a rupee devoted to railways, dams, machine tools, or other tangible capital goods."

Our first job, it seems to me, is to have a clear picture of what we want our educational methods to achieve. The democratic system is not based on producing merely a useful skill for the state; it means the development of a human being to his fullest potentiality, the growth of a complete human being.

Ability is not something to be saved, like money, in the hope that you can draw interest on it. The interest comes from the spending. Unused ability, like unused muscles, will atrophy. It is tragic to realize that the majority of human beings, even the so-called educated, call upon only the smallest fraction of their potential capacity. They leave many talents dormant. They fail to develop their mental qualities. They are almost unaware of the degree of energy upon which they might call to build a full and rewarding life.

Human resources are the most valuable assets the world has. They are all needed desperately. Certainly for the young person the discovery of his own unsuspected capacity is an exciting, a liberating experience.

We cannot deny that we have failed most dismally to achieve this result of helping our young people to develop their maximum capacity. In an increasingly complex world how are we to alter our approach to the problem and do a better job of educational preparation for life?

In the first place, I think we must start with the realization that there is scarcely a subject in any field of knowledge today that has not become so complex that it is impossible for a student to grasp it all. What then? The revolution must come in our whole approach to training the child. The ultimate aim must be to produce trained minds. Since we cannot hope to cover any subject in its entirety, and certainly not a wide range of them, we must, instead, teach the young how to learn and where to find the information they need. The mind must be trained, rather than the memory. It is not subjects so much as methods of learning that must be taught. The mind must be forged as an efficient working tool, so that education will be a continuing process, rather than a matter of learning by rote.

We must, of course, teach the basic skills—reading, writing, and arithmetic. I say "of course," and yet, as a result of recent methods of teaching, these basic skills appear to be deteriorating. Through the right kind of reading, education becomes a continuing process. The person, and there are far too many, who becomes "too busy to have time for a book," has permitted his education to come to a dead stop. Of all the nations in the Western world, the United States, with the most money and the most time, has the fewest readers of books per capita. This is an incalculable loss.

This, too, is one of the few civilized nations in the world which is unable to support a single magazine devoted solely to books.

The reading of books should be a constant voyage of exploration, of adventure, of excitement. The habit of reading is man's bulwark against loneliness, his window opening on life, his unending delight. It is also an open door onto all the paths of knowledge and experience and beauty. But it should never be a chore. Reading should be an experience or it is nothing. As Robert Louis Stevenson said, "To miss the joy is to miss all."

Wide and catholic reading is the foundation of all continued growth in education. But this should reach out as far as possible. It is not enough to read in one field. It is not enough to devote all one's reading time to nonfiction, on the theory that one will find useful facts. Feelings, too, are facts. Emotion is a fact. Human experience is a fact. It is often possible to gain more real insight into human beings and their motivations by reading great fiction than by personal acquaintance. People reveal comparatively little about their inmost natures even to their closest friends.

Democracy and ignorance do not go together. The good citizen is an informed citizen. It is not enough to love democracy and to believe in it. The citizen has to understand it, to be familiar with his institutions and with his history. He has to be able to read—*and to think for himself about what he reads.*

To think for himself. That is the operative phrase. Unlike the indoctrinated Soviet youth, he has to be able to make his own judgments about the truth and the value of statements made to him. He has to weigh them against other statements. He has to see how they fit in with his own observation and with his own sense of values.

Russia, of course, has not been the only country to use education for the purpose of molding thought rather than developing it. When one remembers the educational system in Germany before and during the Second World War, one is aware of how intensively that education, brilliant as it was in many ways, was used for indoctrination. The young men who came out of the German universities were already conditioned to accept, without criticism, the most unspeakable dictatorship of the modern world.

In the long run, I believe, the basic contest of the future will not be settled by bombs but by the amount and quality of education; by the quality of leadership to be developed in the next decade or two. Often, in my talks with college students, I have been struck by the fact that few of them seem to know what they are or what their potentialities, where they are going or how, what they ought to do about themselves, their lives, their relations to their government and to the world.

Certainly the person who does not know where he is going or how to get there is not the material out of which leaders are made. He is too apt to become the led, the passive and supine, unable to choose his own course. Here, more than in any area perhaps, we see clearly the failure of our educational system, for it is the job of education to help orient the student and develop his natural gifts to help him decide where he is going and why.

In any discussion of the problem of education in this country, it is as unfair as it is untrue to lay all the blame for our manifest shortcomings on the school system itself, as though our educational methods were a kind of abstraction and education a detached element functioning in a vacuum.

Education is what the American people have made it or failed to make it. We cannot blame methods we permit to exist for the fact that our young people are uninformed, incurious, vague about themselves and their world. We cannot blame education if our young people are apt to be timid, unadventurous, actually afraid, or beset by crippling self-pity.

How much are the parents contributing to the cause of adequate education? This brings us face to face with a startling fact. There are some eleven million adults in the United States who cannot read so much as a traffic sign!

I am often told by young people in the universities, and told rather resentfully, that it's unfair they have to cope with a world they never made. But this is the common lot of man. What I think they tend to forget is that the world they hand on to their children will be a world they *have* made. If they do not like their inheritance, at least they have every opportunity to improve on it. And that, I feel most strongly, is the great adventure of life, an adventure renewed for every generation. I should like to see our young people face with enjoyment the fact that they are going to have to go along uncharted paths. I should like them to be filled with confidence at meeting new challenges.

Whether or not they have made the world they live in, the young must learn to be at home in it, to be familiar with it. They must understand its history, its peoples, their customs and ideas and problems and aspirations. Let me repeat, *The world cannot be understood from a single point of view.*

One of the most absurd situations today is that we first became aware of our own inadequacies in education when Russia sent its sputnik into space. What, we wondered, had our scientists been doing while this was going on? At this juncture we have too great a tendency to regard the whole all-embracing subject of education as though it were merely a tool for competing with the Russians.

Of course, it would be intelligent of us to take a look at the educational methods of every country, to find what we can learn from them. Victor Cousin, a French philosopher, once said, "The true greatness of a people does not consist in borrowing nothing from others, but in borrowing from all whatever is good, and in perfecting whatever is appropriate."

Perhaps we have put too great an emphasis on the Russian system. I have, in the past, spent much time in Russia studying its educational methods. There are features from which we could doubtless profit. There are features which we should avoid like the plague.

There is one objective, however, that seems to me invaluable. The Russians study the potentialities of every child so that no talent, no ability, no skill may be wasted. Talent in music, in art, and especially, of course, in science, is recognized as early as possible and every opportunity is given for its development. Schooling is taken seriously; it is, indeed, a grim discipline. Hours of work are long; the students, on the whole, learn more in a shorter number of years than they do here.

Actually, this is true of many other countries. While in the United States it takes sixteen years to go through grammar school, high school, and college, this same amount of work on the Continent is done in twelve years. This does not mean that our young people are slower to learn; it means that less is required of them in a given amount of time; their school day is shorter; their school year is much shorter.

In Denmark, for instance, the school year consists of 280 days as compared with 180 days in our country. In other words, a Danish child gets the equivalent of fourteen of our school years in only nine.

What this amounts to is that many of our young people are still going to school well into their middle twenties, a period when the creative process is supposed to be at its peak and they could be putting their energies to use in the job or the profession of their choice.

Here is where the influence of parents is most insidious. We know, for instance, that highly organized college sports are an American phenomenon. Other nations find athletic exercise for everyone more desirable, on the theory of a sound mind in a sound body. But in this country the parents' overdeveloped interest in sports too often leads to professionalism and to a situation where an athletic coach receives much more money than a professor.

It is the parent who urges his friends to "take it easy." It is the parent who seeks fewer hours to devote to his life's work. It is the parent who refers to his profession as "the rat race." But why this implied contempt for the work and the companions of his free choice? Even, it must be supposed, for himself.

These constantly reiterated ideas are not calculated to stir a young person into working longer hours and with shorter vacations in order to equip himself for his job in life, or to respect it. The parent sunk in apathetic viewing of a television screen is not providing an example of the use of the human mind.

Too often, American parents are apt to shrug off the whole problem of our educational inadequacies by stating that, after all, ours is the best system in the world. They point out that the Russians don't teach initiative or individual enterprise.

Well, honestly, are we doing that now? It has seemed to me increasingly over the years that our schools are so involved with problems of what they call "life adjustment" that the net result is to train a child to fit into the group, to teach him conformity; in other words, to prepare him, without pain, to become an organization man.

One obvious area of improvement in education is in the learning of foreign languages. We must revolutionize our teaching of languages, and begin with the earliest grades, when children learn languages as naturally as they breathe. The world of the future is a world of international contact on a wider and wider scale. And communication, after all, is largely a matter of words.

At one time, it was not thought important to learn languages. It was unlikely that our young people would go to other countries. Today, of course, this is no longer true. The traffic highways of the skies are more and more crowded as people go from country to country, from continent to continent, as visitors, as businessmen, as government representatives.

The need for communication is rapidly becoming intensified. Even though some meeting of minds can be achieved through the use of interpreters, there cannot be the same insights, the same sympathy and understanding as when there is no language barrier. There is enormous value in being able to speak the language of the peoples among whom you are to work or live, even when you are only a brief visitor. The use of the other person's language is a friendly gesture and a proof that you are genuinely interested in him and his culture.

What we need first is to provide tools through which languages can be learned easily. The Russians do this better than we do. They teach Latin and Greek and they begin teaching at the time when the child first goes to school. Each child acquires one language of his own choice; it may be German, Chinese, English—with either a British or American accent. By the time he has finished ten years of schooling he speaks and reads and understands that language as well as he does his own. He is equally at home in it.

By the time he reaches higher education he is given what I call a capitalistic incentive, though Mr. Khrushchev disagreed with my use of the term. The student is given a subsistence allowance. The Soviets do not feel that a family should be required to pay for higher education. This should be the duty of the state, they argue, because the state cannot afford to waste any human material and is constantly on the lookout for latent ability which can be developed.

Granted, the subsistence allowance provides rather dull living. But, if the student learns a second foreign language, an additional 20 percent is added to his allowance. If he learns a third one, 15 percent is added. For each new one after that he gets 10 percent more.

Now, once you have mastered the technique of learning languages, they become progressively easier to acquire. As a result of developing this skill of languages more and more people in the Soviet Union are able to talk to more and more people in the world.

In one respect, it seems to me, the Soviets are providing an essential aid to higher education, through government support. In this country too many young people who are capable of higher education must forgo it because of lack of funds. It is my belief that the American government should supply funds for college as well as the public-school education.

Here I should like to use my husband's favorite quotation from Abraham Lincoln: "The legitimate object of Government is to do for a community of people whatever they need to have done but cannot do at all or cannot do so well for themselves in their separate capacities."

Another area in which we have fallen seriously behind is in the teaching of history, not only the history of the world but the history of our own country. How can we expect our young people to vote intelligently when they do not understand the principles upon which their own country is based, when they are unfamiliar with the events that have shaped its existence? Without this knowledge how can they understand the relationship of their country to the world at a time of world upheaval?

The Russians, in contrast, give their children a basic understanding of their philosophy of government. They also train them to be prepared to answer criticisms of their system which they may encounter abroad.

Of course, this training entails disadvantages we should avoid like the plague. One of the greatest, from the American standpoint, is that, like our young Birchite, the Soviets feel that "a university is no place for controversial ideas." The range of free thought, the ability to lay hands on free information, is restricted. History is taught with a bland disregard for truth. Economics is taught as part of the dogma of Marxism. From babyhood the child's mind is shaped and molded to fit a certain pattern of ideas.

One thing must be clear to everyone. You cannot prepare any young person to meet the conditions of his world if you falsify the history that he is taught. Russia is not the only sinner in this respect. Even today, children in Germany are not being taught the truth about Hitler and the regime which changed the face of Europe.

Have we given our schoolchildren man's noblest freedom— freedom from fear?

For some years an unpleasant and unattractive attitude has been developed in our young people. They seem to be losing their sense of adventure, their courage, their zest in the face of the future. The British novelist W. Somerset Maugham, who was in the United States for some months during the Second World War, was greatly struck by the unadventurous spirit of the American youth. It seemed to him that all they wanted was to land in a secure job in an office somewhere, take no chances, and surrender any personal sense of responsibility.

There was, it is true, during the period of Senator McCarthy, a startling lesson for the young. They learned that any comment, any action taken, might in later years be brought up against them. As a result, too many of them grew afraid to express or even to hold an opinion of their own. Time after time, I have encountered this characteristic of timid withdrawal, this desire for security without responsibility. One can understand it in the old and weary. In the young it is fatal.

Frequently, too frequently, when I talk to college students I am met with the same questions: "Why should we plan to marry and have children and build a career and plan our lives? The Bomb may destroy mankind. There's no security ahead. What's the use?"

I would have them go back and read Bradford's reply to the people who hesitated in Holland before risking the great adventure into the unknown of the Plymouth colonists. The answer, of course, is that there never has been safety. There never has been security. No man has ever known what he would meet around the next corner; if life were predictable it would cease to be life, and be without flavor.

The answer to fear is not to cower and hide; it is not to surrender feebly without contest. The answer is to stand and face it boldly. Look at it, analyze it, and, in the end, act.

With action, confidence grows. I am convinced that one of the reasons why our young people today feel uncertain is that they are not being trained to examine questions, to decide for themselves on a method of action—*and then to act*. The result is that they may too easily be acted upon.

All this brings us to the necessity of a revolution in teaching teachers. One of the most important things we have to do at the present time is to intensify our search for really fine teachers. We have done so much to intimidate our teachers, to belittle their position in the community, to discourage their thinking independently, to underpay them, to bind them to the attitudes of school boards with narrow limitations that it is most unfair now to expect them to be prepared to meet the new conditions.

It seems to me that it would be a sound idea to begin where the core of responsibility lies—with the school boards. Their work should be closely scrutinized; their ability to provide adequate education should be analyzed. Is there any reason why members of school boards should not take yearly refresher courses in problems of modern education just as teachers are expected to continue and renew their education?

Occasionally we find a truly great teacher, one who is able to arouse curiosity, to stir excitement, to generate ideas, to open wide the windows on new vistas and the doors on new pathways. Such teachers are beyond price. But for the most part we have hundreds who have little or no conception of their job beyond daily drilling in subject matter or the use of teaching methods. There are few who can impart any great interest. There are fewer who make a study of their students and their potentialities. There are fewer still who have any idea of what preparation the young need for the great tasks of the future.

And this appears to be true at all levels. An eleven-year-old boy was talking with me lately. During his summer vacation he had read fifty books of his own choice and for his own pleasure. But, he pointed out, his teacher wasn't interested in books. Now and then she assigned one as a chore to be got through, a lesson to be learned, and then had no real interest in whether or not he had liked it or what he had thought of it.

"She's not even a good baby sitter," Bill said in disgust.

The time has long since passed, it seems to me, for education to be haphazard. Without delay we should set up standards that must be fulfilled. For instance, a high-school diploma should represent a certain clearly defined amount of knowledge. Every year, thirty-five million people in the United States move from one section to another, from one state to another. Their children are subjected to many kinds of standards in education, depending entirely upon the state or the particular school for the quality of education they receive, for the value of the particular high-school diploma they happen to earn.

This is most unfair to our children. Standards in food and drugs are rigidly enforced. Does it matter so little what goes into the minds in comparison with what goes into the stomachs?

Another advantage of establishing standards—and much higher standards—is that, inevitably, a rise in teaching standards must follow as the night the day.

Vice Admiral Hyman G. Rickover declared bluntly, some months ago at a Congressional hearing, "My visit to Russia and Poland confirmed my belief that the real race we are in with Communism is to see whose educational system best prepares youth for the world of modern science and technology."

Today, the Soviets are graduating 120,000 scientists annually. We are graduating only 40,000.

Every day we postpone improving and upgrading our education is a day's advance for the Soviets. How long can we permit Congress to hold us back?

7.

GETTING TO KNOW YOU

"When I use a word," Humpty-Dumpty said in a rather
scornful tone, "it means just what I choose it to mean, neither more nor less."

"The question is," said Alice, "whether you *can* make
words mean different things."

"The question is," said Humpty-Dumpty, "which is to be
master—that's all."

LEWIS CARROLL

On a summer afternoon the picnic grounds back of my Hyde
Park cottage held as colorful a throng of people as have ever
been there. There were young people from most of the countries of the world who were here to study the democratic
process. There were Nigerians in brilliant costumes and
dramatic headdresses; there were saris like bright tulips on
the lawn. There were Africans, Indians, Chinese, Japanese,
Europeans.

What one noticed, after the first impression of gaiety and
color and the drama of exotic costume, was how different
from each other all these young people seemed. Then, when
they had finished their picnic lunch and were still widely scattered around the lawn, a young man began to strum on a guitar the Rodgers and Hammerstein song "Getting to Know
You."

Little by little, the group drew closer together; slowly and
rather shyly, the voices joined in until the chorus rang out
triumphantly.

After the guitar had been put down and the song died away, we talked. There were many accents, many degrees of education, many points of view. And I discovered then, as I think they all discovered, not that they were different, but that they were very alike. They had the same human aspirations, the same dreams, the same longing for a good life. Perhaps they had more than the average young person, for this group was inspired as well by a desire to make life better for their own lands and their own peoples. They had already begun to learn the lesson that we must all learn from each other. They had already begun to learn that we are united by our aspirations and divided only by our fears, many of them artificially and deliberately created. But they had taken the first step toward conquering or defying those fears. They were getting to know one another.

One of the most important things for our young people to learn is the difficult art of being at home in the world. Ahead of them lies the gigantic, but infinitely rewarding, task of learning to know and understand other peoples, and the equally difficult task of helping other peoples to know and understand them. So far, with the most advanced communications system in the world we have failed in telling our story to the world, in giving other people a real picture of ourselves, our convictions, our principles, our way of life. What is the reason for this? I think there are several major reasons for our stupendous failure to communicate.

The first, it seems to me, is that we have failed to understand the point of view from which we are observed, to take into account the attitudes of other people and to respect them.

Let me illustrate this point with a story. A few months ago, one of my grandsons returned from Tanganyika, where he had spent a summer in a famine area. The job he had been given was to distribute food, American corn, over one hundred miles of territory. In return for the food, the people of the villages were asked to build earthen dams that would hold rain water in gulleys so that, another year, they would have water for irrigation.

In preparation for the journey he had learned Swahili, but

he discovered, in dismay, that every village had a different dialect, so he took with him an interpreter who could bridge the language gaps.

He is, like most young Americans, impatient and eager to get things done. His hundred-mile territory was going, he realized, to be slow work. There were no roads and it took three hours to travel fifteen miles. He was in a hurry by the time he reached the first village. He tried to get the people to go to work on their dams without delay. No one moved.

What was wrong? He urged the interpreter to hurry them up. The interpreter refused. Before doing anything else, he explained, the people wanted to hold a welcoming ceremony. In spite of their famished state, they presented my grandson with a token of bread and salt. There ensued a lengthy conversation. They asked him about the health and welfare of every member of his family. Then, when they had finished, he, prompted by the interpreter, asked detailed questions about them, their children, their parents, their aunts and uncles.

After that the peoples set to with a will, working gaily and enthusiastically to build their small dams.

"It was an eye opener to me," he confessed.

Because their ways were not his ways it had been easy to criticize, to try to prod them into action, to ride roughshod over their customs and point of view. But there was a reason for their behavior. That exchange of information about their families had been a form of graciousness, a desire to establish some personal understanding, some recognition of each other as human beings. When this had been achieved, they got the work done fast and cheerfully. From this exchange the people had gained food and a possible water supply. What my grandson had gained was a real respect and understanding for the ways of another civilization.

The most important point here is that the benefit was mutual. I have always felt pretty sure that if you are doing something that exploits people and is purely selfish they will always know it. But if you act from a real concern for people, a desire to help them to develop themselves, you will find warm cooperation and eventually an ability to work together that is fruitful because it is voluntary and not imposed. But it must be a natural growth based on mutual respect and trust.

Long ago, de Tocqueville commented that Americans reasoned by trying to explain "a mass of facts by a single cause." And again I must emphasize, *The world cannot be understood from a single point of view.* I keep repeating this because this is one of our blind spots as Americans.

Learning to be at home in the world is, I believe, the surest way we have of reducing our fears. For fear, after all, is too often fear of one's inadequacy in the face of the unknown.

The greatest and most inspiring adventure of all time probably will be carried out in the next fifty years, the adventure of building a new world. As our young people come to have a closer and deeper understanding of that world and its peoples, they will learn that there is not one civilization, from the oldest to the very newest, from which we cannot learn. We can learn to appreciate what motivates people, as my grandson learned in Tanganyika. We can learn to understand what they do and, above all, why. From almost all of them there is something we can take that will enrich our lives, which can be adapted to our own uses.

Dealing with people is never a one-way process. It must always be a matter of give-and-take. Our young people must learn to live with other people. If they are going to belong to a world society they must be trained to cope with it, neither to follow nor to dominate, but to cooperate as mutually self-respecting human beings.

Now it is true that, in one respect, at least, the newest countries have an advantage which ours does not. The building of a new nation is one of the most inspiring activities that man can know, activating everyone from the smallest child to the oldest grandfather. This particular excitement of self-expression can be seen best, perhaps, today in the state of Israel. There you see everyone working, stirred by participation in a common cause for a single goal.

I remember well, in the state's earliest days, going to a children's village which was built on top of a rocky hill. Down in the valley there was a little garden and in every hollow among the rocks the children had planted something. One small boy showed me a first small shoot of green.

"I am growing food for Israel," he told me proudly.

This feeling of contributing to a common cause and to the common welfare is a tremendous incentive. It is not one that has been instilled into our own young people. They feel that our country is so thoroughly developed that no individual contribution is of any particular importance. There is no way, it seems to them, in which their personal efforts can make any real contribution.

It is up to all of us to help change this concept. We must make our young people realize that their job of the future is not only to help continue to strengthen their nation along traditional lines, but to try to discover new ways in which they may eventually build a new world in which people can live at peace.

One of our stumbling blocks is that the young can retort, and with too much truth, that we have set them a poor example. The United States has found itself a world power almost by accident, yet Americans, by and large, still remain reluctant to assume their international responsibility. Why then, the young ask, should they be expected to make the future welfare of the world a matter of their personal responsibility?

The only answer to that, of course, is that democracy requires a sense of personal involvement, of personal responsibility, of personal courage. We ask them to learn by our mistake but to remember the faith many of us have tried to live by.

By and large, the sum total of this nation's foreign policy is the combined voice of its people. Our impact on the rest of the world is the sum total of what each of us does as a private citizen. We tell citizens in foreign lands what kind of people we are by what we do here.

Every individual can function productively in the small area in which he lives. If he functions according to the principles on which this nation was founded—courage, integrity, fearlessness, conviction—he will help his community to develop along those lines. Indeed, if he develops a real understanding of his own community, of the variety of its people, of the variety of their problems, he will find before long that his interest has extended to the next community and the one beyond that; he will look beyond his state to its relation with his country; and the relation of his country with the world.

I believe that we, as a people, are apt to profit more by the work of the Peace Corps than are the countries which the Peace Corps groups are attempting to help. When these people—most of them young—return to us it will be with a wider and deeper knowledge and respect for the peoples among whom they have worked, a knowledge which they can bring back and share with us.

Not long ago, a group of Peace Corps workers came to see me. These were dedicated young men and women, of a high intellectual level.

"What has your training given you?" I asked them.

"When I came here," one of them replied, "I thought I would be told how to approach the secondary-school students I was going to teach. What I have learned is that I have to do this myself. That startled me at first. I realize that I must learn to be much more sensitive about what other people think and feel."

A young woman said, "My training has given me a feeling for the need for understanding, and for progressing slowly until I feel sure about the extent of my understanding."

One of the best features of the Peace Corps is that its members are required to live in the ways of the people of the country to which they are going, and on the same economic level. This not only intensifies their understanding of the problems but it prevents them from being set apart because they live under different conditions.

When one thinks of the millions of American soldiers who have been stationed all over the world, one realizes that they could have done much to spur such understanding. But their pay was high, their way of life superior, so that they often aroused resentment and were rarely in a position to know the people at first hand.

When we consider that these soldiers were often risking

their lives for the people among whom they were stationed, the waste and tragedy of the situation become even more apparent. The savior, the protector, became merely the stranger, the invader. There were, of course, many many cases of individual soldiers who became warm friends of the people among whom they lived, but they remained the exceptions, not the rule.

Next year, the Peace Corps is to be increased to ten thousand. What I should like to see is a way of continuing to use the information and understanding its members bring back from other lands. I should like to see these young people used in schools scattered around the country, or be on a kind of loan basis to other countries where their experience might be needed.

In fact, I should like to see a sort of bank of human talent set up by means of which young American doctors or accountants, engineers or shoemakers, teachers or truck drivers, farmers or scientists, might be loaned to the countries that required their services.

One of my warnings to the Peace Corps members who called on me last summer was: "Tell the truth about us, wherever you go. Don't lie to make the picture brighter than life. Don't claim that we have no failures. But do explain why we have our successes and what they are."

It was John Milton who spoke of "our greatest merchandise— truth." With all our shortcomings, the truth about America carries its own force. When young people—or, indeed, people of all ages—come to this country and look at it for themselves, they see how democracy functions in daily life; see men and women going about their lives without fear, in fields they have chosen.

On most of them the effect is staggering. So much that we take for granted seems incredible to them. And here, indeed, the Russians have no comparable thing to offer. In their country, visitors are taken on conducted tours to see what they are permitted to see. But what they see is a disciplined people, fixed in the lot to which they have been assigned. Even with our failures to solve our race problem, even with prejudice and injustice and occasional brutality shown in the South, we still have a glowing picture to offer.

It is not chance that, in spite of desperate wooing by the Soviets, not one of the forty-two new nations in Africa has committed itself to Communism.

One reason why Khrushchev keeps up agitation about East and West Berlin is that the divided city provides the strongest object lesson to be found anywhere in the practical results of the two great ways of life. Take a stroll through the dark, stark, impoverished, dominated section of East Berlin followed by one through West Berlin, alight, vigorous, prosperous, free. There is the picture in a nutshell. It is a picture we should bear in mind. Certainly Mr. Khrushchev never forgets it.

It has always been my conviction that example is the best evidence one can produce. Here is the strength of the Peace Corps. Its members provide a practical demonstration of what can be done, not in terms of our degree of civilization, *but in terms of the immediate needs of the people they serve.* I think we will be astonished at the rapidity with which many of the natives living along the African coast will develop with these new but simple techniques, and how quickly these new methods will change the thinking of bush people in the interior whom we have regarded as centuries behind us.

On the other hand, it would be unreasonable for us to expect a complete change of thinking overnight. In *The Interplay of East and West,* Barbara Ward points this out:

"I cannot resist quoting one example from West Africa of the complexity of this mixture. If plans drawn up for a new dam and its reservoir involve the flooding-over of the sites of local fetishes, then a calculation has to be made of the income necessary to propitiate and compensate the fetish priests and this income must be covered in the final cost of electricity."

Because our young Peace Corps people are living on the same level as the people among whom they are working, much of the hostility, the clash of cultures, will cease to exist. To have shared a couple of years in close contact with the people of these different areas will provide a completely new concept of how to deal with situations which are beyond our own ken and which are often not understandable even to the people with whom we are working.

Our top people in the State Department frequently have to rely on reports from diplomatic officials who have been trained but not always to be close observers of other civilizations. Now the department is going to have a body of observers who have really lived with people who are different from themselves, and have been able to acquire the understanding and genuine interest that can only come from such close association.

There is, it seems to me, a second major way in which we have failed to communicate with the peoples of the world. Because we are proud of our high standard of living, we frequently make propaganda use of the wrong features of our life. We boast to the impoverished of our luxurious living. We stress our materialistic values, our "success" shibboleths, to people for whom they have little meaning but who have instead high spiritual values. We describe our aggressive drives to "get ahead" to nonaggressive people. "Get ahead of whom?" they wonder in some alarm.

Here is another evidence of our shortcomings in education: Too often we send young people and the not so young to foreign countries without having prepared them to meet the questions they will inevitably be asked about our form of government, our way of life, our values. They fumble and often find themselves unable to answer questions to which they should know the answers.

Too often, we stress what we "give" them and then are both hurt and angry when they show neither gratitude nor complete trust. Why should they? They are as clearly aware as we are that we are seeking their backing, that any dealing we have with them is for our mutual welfare.

Then again, we give the impression of trying to compete with Russia on Russia's terms. We do not sound like people with a vibrant democratic faith of our own, going steadily toward a goal in which we believe with all our hearts.

In many ways we tell the wrong story to the world. We make

no real effort to reply to the consistently dishonest picture of its accomplishments that Russia has given to the new nations. Are we, I wonder, making any attempt to point out the areas of Russia's weaknesses? Let's take a look at some of them:

1. After all these years they still dare not expose their people to Western ideas.
2. The divided city of Berlin provides an object lesson to the world in contrasts. The Berlin wall had to be constructed to prevent the people of the East from escaping the Communist regime. In recent years, more than a million people have come West, some of them at terrible risk.
3. In spite of all their wooing, no African nation has joined them. Their satellites were conquered by force of arms and their so-called "liberation" has fooled nobody.
4. Today, the Common Market countries have more money, more prosperity, more potential military manpower than Soviet Russia.
5. Satellite countries, like colonies, are not economically sound; they produce less and they cost more to control than do free people.
6. Their training does not develop free minds and therefore cannot produce independent leaders.
7. The Russians dare not permit visitors to view for themselves the conditions of their country as a whole, while even our bad spots prove to the visitor to be infinitely better than he has been told.
8. The tragic story of Hungary's abortive uprising has given the lie to the Soviet propaganda about their desire to be communized.

There is no doubt, too, that the Russian people still live at a level far below that of the vast majority of Western countries. The shop windows look attractive but there is little or nothing to buy inside. Clothing is so costly as to be almost prohibitive. A man will work four weeks to earn the price of a pair of shoes. One day I looked out on Moscow Square and noticed that every man and woman had on shiny new rubber boots.

I asked about this strange phenomenon. The people were working on a government project, I was told, and they had all been given rubber boots, which were very rare and much prized.

Housing improves constantly in Russia but it would seem intolerable to people of the West to live, as the Soviets must, without privacy. Space is rigidly allotted according to the size of the family, regardless of position or income. A family of six has three rooms.

So long as Russia's major effort goes into scientific and military programs that stretch their resources to the limit, the people will continue to be forced to sacrifice personal comfort.

We so often hear criticism at home because we do not seem to be understood in different parts of the world. I think it is important we try to figure out for ourselves why this is.

As a whole, the people whom we are addressing with our communications system live in poverty and many of them are ridden by disease. They look at our remarkable system and hear what we say abroad. But they look at us from a condition of perpetual hunger, from a life that is an unending battle for subsistence, a constant struggle that offers few alleviations.

Let us remember the eyes that look at us from this background and then try to imagine what our own reactions would be if we were in their position. Perhaps we would then wonder whether these people can understand why Americans advertise what we spend in a year for cosmetics. Yet that is one of our recurrent boasts.

We like to brag about our ways of spending money to people who, if they hope to get the most elementary education, must make fantastic sacrifices. Is it any wonder that when they hear we are loath to spend money for improvement in education or that we fight against giving economic aid to underdeveloped nations, they have a certain cynical feeling about how much real sacrifice we are willing to make for a better world? They know what we spend because, being an open country, we publish our assets and accomplishments, our figures and our costs. They know what we spend on space programs, on military security.

And then they hear of great difficulties in solving our racial problems. They wonder, two-thirds of the people of the world being colored, whether we really have the arrogance to believe that white people should have all the privileges of the earth. They hear that in this land where, on the whole, the standard of living, of health, of opportunity is very high, there are unemployment and distressed areas where poverty exists almost equal to theirs. They wonder about the degree of real intelligence in people who cannot solve these problems when they have so much of this world's goods and so few basic worries.

They understand that there is food in this country, food enough for everybody, too much food, and that some people are hungry because they cannot pay for it. To them this seems like poor management. We must have forgotten to plan.

These are the things we have to remember as we think about how people look at us. Why should they feel very grateful for what we do for them? It must be remembered that our major foreign aid is in military weapons, mostly those we have discarded. We give the weapons on the assumption that these nations may be strengthened in standing out against a Soviet attack. Of course, the chance that they could stand up against such an attack is most unlikely. We fool ourselves as far as that is concerned.

When it comes to the other programs, is it very astonishing if they wonder whether we are trying to buy their good will? Most of the countries of the world have been trading with the United States ever since sailing ship days. And we were always hard traders. They hear tales about great organizations like the United Fruit Company owning the governments and controlling the economics of the countries in which they operate.

All these things and many more could be given as examples of some of the difficulties that we have in making people accept us as the kind of people we really are. We are very decent people, very generous on the whole, although what we have given has cost the individual taxpayer little.

Perhaps the most bewildering thing other people hear about us is that we are afraid of the Soviets. This is astonishing to them. We have so much and yet we are afraid of a nation that has to bleed its people in order to keep up with us. We seem to have no assurance that our values and dreams and beliefs and purposes are capable of coping with the Soviets.

Lately, we have allowed the Soviets to put us in a position of answering their challenge rather than finding ways in which we would be challenging them. They think up ways of persuading people in the world to believe in them. We assume that if people want to know about us they can come here and find out. We do not try to draw them in. True, we offer a few scholarships and when the students come we let them study, but often they never see the inside of an American home.

And here I should like to tell a story—a true story, I am profoundly sorry to say—that illustrates how not to try to create a picture of American generosity.

After the Second World War a young Japanese girl won a scholarship to study for a year in an American university; the requirements for the scholarship were high and the competition was strenuous. As it happened, this girl was the daughter of one of Japan's most distinguished professional men. She had lived in considerable luxury, in a household with many servants, until the American bombing of Tokyo had destroyed everything her father possessed—except, oddly enough, for a single book, an American book.

Well, the Japanese girl came to the United States and attended college for a year. Her record was so brilliant, her grades were so high, that the scholarship was renewed for a second year. But how was she to maintain herself during the intervening summer months?

A wealthy American woman heard of the case and offered to have the girl come to her home as her guest for the summer. Not only that, she gave interviews to the press, proclaiming her own generosity in doing so. In fact, she gained a great deal of publicity for herself. But—and this she did not publicize— she let her house servants go for that summer and put her Japanese "guest" to work to earn her room and board.

This would have been unattractive enough, as an act of essential dishonesty, but what was also involved was the Oriental question of face. The girl from a rigid class system had been put in an intolerable and, in her eyes, shameful position, all in the guise of American hospitality.

So here we have the case of a young girl who had been given two years in an American college, two years in which a link of friendship could grow between two nations that, so short a time before, had been at war with each other. But the net result was a sense of bitterness and disillusionment. One woman's selfish vanity, her desire for personal publicity, her willingness to make blatant and unscrupulous use of another person had destroyed all that might have been accomplished.

This is only one example of the kind of selfish stupidity we sometimes indulge in. I could multiply it a thousand times. For instance, how many of us bother to find out whether there are any foreign students near us, so that we can make them feel at home in our country, make them like us and understand our ways? Too many of these students are brought over to American colleges and then never have an opportunity to make a single American friend during their period of residence. This is shortsighted. It is, in fact, stupid; particularly when, as most often happens, the foreign student belongs to one of the so-called colored races.

It is not coincidence that many former students in American colleges were later among the Japanese officers who were guilty of such ferocious torture of American prisoners. They were, from their standpoint, repaying humiliations they had encountered at the hands of prejudiced Americans in the past.

Surely we ought to take the trouble to explain our problems in achieving integration of the races in this country. Very few foreigners understand our unusual system of state and federal rights. They do not realize that there are areas in which the state has complete jurisdiction.

This factor looms large, too, in our work in the United Nations. Not many of the foreign delegates ever understand that in this country the power lies in the hands of the people, who have delegated some of it to their state representatives, and have assigned certain other carefully limited powers to the federal government. We do not have the simple problem of one single voice. We have fifty, often conflicting, voices to be heard—and heeded.

There is one vital area of communications where we seem to be going out of the way to damage the picture other people have of us. This is in the field of the books and the movies which represent us abroad. I wonder how many Americans have any idea of the effect of most of this material when it is viewed by outsiders.

There was a time when our literature gave a fairly well-rounded picture of us as a nation, of our strength and our weaknesses, the good and the bad, but always within a framework of the principles on which our society was based. But shortly after the First World War a new cult grew up, the cult of *The Waste Land*, of *The Hollow Men*, of life and mankind bankrupt of dignity or meaning.

Writers all over America began to describe us as a nation of gangsters, of the corrupt, of the self-seeking, of the sterile and the greedy, of the sick and the degenerate. Now, of course, all these elements exist. They exist everywhere in the world. But if they were preponderant in this country we could not have continued to grow as we have; our people would not be living, as they do for the most part, in peaceful and well-run communities. This was only a small part of the truth, but it was, too often, the only part the rest of the world was shown.

The same thing applies, to an even greater degree, to many of the movies we have sent abroad. Americans at home can see them, knowing the whole picture. But to people in other lands this is a faithful portrayal of what we are, what we believe, where our values lie.

What we must do, it seems to me, is to keep the balance clear, the values straight. For example, there is much truth in *The Ugly American*. I myself could point to certain individuals and say that I recognize the unfortunate kind of foreign representative described in that book. But these represent only a small fraction. I can point, too, to many dedicated men and women who have given years of their lives to the study and understanding of other areas of the world, people whose integrity and unselfish devotion to their work is beyond cavil.

And while we are on the subject of the books that represent us, I must point out that we are not yet making the effort we should to get them into the hands of the impoverished peoples of the world. In the first place we send few books, often badly selected. In the second place, these are often sold at a price completely beyond the means of the people. In the third place, too many of them are in English and therefore have a limited audience. In contrast, the Soviets are literally flooding these countries with books, in their own languages and priced in pennies. They are, moreover, designed for the degree of education and civilization of the people whom the Russians want to reach.

We in the United States have become so intoxicated by our new methods of communication that we have failed to look closely at just what we are communicating—or failing to communicate. If people do not understand us we think it must be their fault.

This is a poor time for misunderstanding. Let us acquaint ourselves with the people to whom we speak so that we can address them in terms that have meaning for them. And then we can provide them, in Milton's noble words, with "our greatest merchandise—truth."

8.

THE MACHINERY FOR PEACE

Humanity with all its fears,
With all its hopes of future years,
Is hanging breathless on thy fate.

HENRY WADSWORTH LONGFELLOW

Today, every human being in the world stands in constant peril from irresponsible use of nuclear power. But today, also, we have created the only machinery for peace that has ever functioned. That, of course, is the United Nations. The only real hope we can have of the survival of the human race lies in showing this new generation coming along how to improve that machinery to prevent our self-destruction.

If we go back in history we can find plenty of instances of civilizations that grew, flourished, and died. They died because human beings did not have the breadth of vision to understand the needs for human survival.

Because it is the work of men and women, of fallible human beings, the United Nations is not a perfect instrument. *But it is all we have.* If we are conscious of its imperfections then it is up to us, to every one of us, to try to find workable ways of improving it. I am reminded of Benjamin Franklin at the Constitutional Convention. There was, perhaps, not a single man there who approved wholeheartedly of that great document. But it was all they had. And Franklin begged any man who did not like some of its features to doubt his own infallibility a little and accept it.

One of the great stumbling blocks in the acceptance of our Constitution, of course, was the jealous clashes and distrust between state and federal groups. Everyone was afraid of having to give up a little.

At present the chief stumbling block in widespread backing of the United Nations is the fear each nation has that it will have to give up a little. In the case of our thirteen American colonies, years passed before the increased strength and benefits for all became truly evident and counteracted jealousy of individual rights and suspicions of group rights. It will doubtless take longer for us to lose our fear and distrust of other nations, other ways of life; to overcome our fear of losing some small part of our sovereignty for the common good, which means, as well, our own good and our own survival.

Suppose that the United States were to withdraw completely from world affairs. What then? Would we have assured our own independence and sovereignty and safety? Certainly not. Instead we would lose the only machinery for peace that exists, while the Communist tide would rise unchecked and the Bomb would still be there.

Any step, however small, that leads to international peace, to universal understanding, to strengthening the machinery of the United Nations is a good step. In fact, it seems to me that before we can ever hope to achieve universal disarmament we must create a climate of psychological disarmament. *The people must want peace* and they must put their weight behind achieving it. It is not alone the few warmongers who create the danger; it is, to a much greater extent, the apathetic.

"There have always been wars," say the cliché-minded. The implication is that wars must always occur in the future. But it would be equally sensible to say, "There have always been plagues and pestilence, smallpox and diphtheria, typhoid fever and other diseases." Yet we know that these are not inevitable and inescapable scourges. We have put our intelligence to work on known facts and consequently rid ourselves of these death dealers. When they occur now it is because of neglect and ignorance. But they do not need to occur at all.

It is curious to look back, from the standpoint of history and its teaching, at the wars that have engaged the Western world during the past two hundred years. As a result of those wars—and war always seems to me a temporary breakdown of civilized values—millions upon millions of human beings have died. And the more "advanced" we have become the more horribly many of them have died.

In each of these wars everyone, on each side, was persuaded that his was the cause of righteousness, that he was wielding a flaming sword against the forces of darkness. And the man against whom he fought stood for all the forces of evil.

But a war ends and there is a shuffle in the cards of power politics. The man who was our enemy is now our friend; the friend at whose side we fought so gladly and so proudly has now become the enemy. From a long-range viewpoint all this appears to be nothing but criminal stupidity.

I am aware that if we commit ourselves wholeheartedly to the strengthening of the United Nations—and I share the opinion of Clark M. Eichelberger that the United Nations should be the foundation of policy, not a diplomatic tool—there will be outcries from people complaining, "That is a risk."

Of course it is.

"How do we know," these people ask, "that the nations of the world will act wisely, that they will not all follow one ideology or another?"

Of course we don't know.

But there is no better course than to put our collective trust in a group of trained people such as one finds in the majority of cases in the United Nations.

In this public forum, whose actions and opinions are heard in every corner of the world, we can put before the world the alternatives and the choices that must be made. We can appeal always to the enormous strength and pressure of public opinion. And this, it seems obvious, is the best risk we could take.

It is the United Nations influence on the opinion of the

world that has made the Soviets so determined to destroy its usefulness if they possibly can. Year after year, we have seen their efforts to render it impotent. Are we then to say meekly, "Oh, the Soviets don't want the United Nations to succeed; they are afraid of what it is accomplishing. Therefore, of course, we'll play along and pay no attention to it either. Let's let the whole thing go"?

In many respects, we still, in this nuclear age, live and think in terms of the past when it comes to international affairs. We are still trying to make the old balance of power work. And yet, under that system, there has not been a day in recorded history when at least a small war was not going on somewhere in the world. In other words, the old system does not work for peace and it is peace we want.

Since the United Nations was set up it has been possible to prevent the outbreak of World War III. In his report to the Fourth General Assembly Secretary-General Trygve Lie said: "United Nations action in other parts of the world has also contributed to the progress made toward a more peaceful world by either preventing or ending wars involving 500,000,000 people."

The effect of collective security was shown by United Nations resistance to aggression at the 38th parallel in Korea. What might easily have turned into a chain of aggressions involving the whole East was prevented.

Now just as changing conditions brought about the need for amendments to our Constitution, so changing conditions altered many of the calculations on which the Charter of the United Nations was based, some of them almost before the ink was dry.

Chief of these, of course, was the dropping of the first atomic bomb on Hiroshima, which altered the original concept of security. A new and incalculable factor had entered the picture.

Little by little, however, the United Nations has proved its capacity for flexibility in coping not only with world conditions but with the recalcitrance of some of its own members, with the deliberate efforts to defeat its objectives, with the changes that have come in its own structure.

This flexibility of the United Nations Charter represents the same kind of strength and capacity for growth that our American Constitution has revealed in the face of change. Chief Justice Marshall wrote of our Constitution that "it was intended to endure for ages to come and to be adapted to the various crises of human affairs."

Like our Constitution, too, the United Nations Charter does not, again in Marshall's words, "attempt to provide, by immutable rules, for exigencies which, if foreseen at all, must have been seen dimly, and which can best be provided as they occur."

Clark M. Eichelberger summed up succinctly the situation as it existed in 1956: "The final break-up of the 5-power system in the United Nations occurred in 1956 when the United Kingdom and France vetoed a resolution in the Security Council over Suez, and the Soviet Union vetoed a resolution urging it to desist from armed intervention in Hungary. These vetoes led to two extraordinary and simultaneous sessions of the General Assembly in which the United States was the only great power willing to assume its Security Council obligations under the Charter in all circumstances."

Now the main point is this. Discouraging as all these circumstances were, did they render the United Nations impotent? Not at all. If the Security Council has declined in authority, the General Assembly has gained in power and influence. When the Security Council is unable to keep the peace because of a veto, the Uniting for Peace Resolution enables the General Assembly to take over.

In 1946, Ambassador Austin stated in an address to the General Assembly: "The General Assembly wields power primarily as the voice of the conscience of the world . . . we foresee a great and expanding area of operations for the General Assembly."

In 1961, Benjamin V. Cohen delivered a series of lectures on the United Nations at Harvard University. He summed up the situation in a telling way: "The effectiveness of the United Nations, however, depends not only on the lettered provisions of the Charter, but more importantly on the will and determination of the nations of the world to make it work, and upon the wisdom, imagination, and resourcefulness that their statesmen bring to that task."

Main sources of conflict in the United Nations obviously have been the admission of new nations and the disarmament problem as it has been complicated by the development of atomic power.

Let's take the difficulties presented by atomic fission first. The unpalatable fact with which we must start is this: If we want to save ourselves—and that means all the world, for fall-out is no respecter of nations or of treaties—we must be willing to accept the restraints that would apply to all nations which have nuclear power. A taboo for one must be a taboo for all. It is fatuous blindness for anyone to assume that the United States or the Soviet Union should have special privileges; that they should be allowed unrestricted freedom in the control or use of this deadly power.

Indeed, we have only two major choices at this time. One is to continue to make bombs, to build nuclear strength for military purposes. Already enough bombs exist to destroy the whole world. We know that this multiplication of weapons of death solves nothing whatever.

The other choice is the complete end of the use of nuclear power for warfare. That means that the United States as well as the Soviets would have to stop building power for themselves.

There is, of course, a third alternative, but this seems to me incredible and unacceptable. It is the suggestion that we merely build bomb shelters and prepare to retire underground. Somehow, I can't see the American people crawling underground like moles looking for safety. I want to be out in the sun and the fresh air. I want everyone to be out there.

The only way we can free ourselves from the fear of the Bomb is to remove it as an instrument of war completely, and that can be done only by placing full control of all nuclear force and intelligence in the hands of an international power, the United Nations.

If the United Nations had control of nuclear weapons we would certainly all be better off than if the United States and the Soviet Union had that control. The United Nations is responsible to the world as a whole and I take it that the world as a whole will be consistently opposed to taking the risk of any kind of nuclear destruction.

But we must learn to swallow the bitter fact that if you want the threat of nuclear war to be controlled, you have to accept the risks of control. The trouble seems to be that while most human beings want peace, they also want to have everything their own way. Something has to give.

It was Bernard Baruch who first presented the plan of the United States for the regulation and control of atomic weapons. This was to be an International Atomic Development Authority, which would have a monopoly of the world's production of atomic energy. It would have the sole authority to engage in atomic research. No other nation at any time has ever made so broad a proposal for a world system of control.

The Soviets rejected the plan as "thoroughly vicious and unacceptable."

Today, however, when no single power can control the activities of the United Nations, it might be wise to press once more for this form of control, which would take atomic power forever out of the hands of belligerent nations interested primarily in their own increase of power and influence.

Today, the voice of the United Nations is heard in every corner of the world. Were the Soviets to reject this kind of control it would give the lie forever to their claims of peaceful intentions.

One thing should be obvious to everyone. We cannot discuss disarmament, we cannot provide for collective security in any meaningful sense as long as we continue to pretend that Red China does not exist. It contains one-fourth of the people of the world. It now has the secret of nuclear power and will, certain scientists have declared, have the Bomb itself—perhaps by the time this book is published.

It is therefore downright idiotic to continue to ignore the existence of this potentially dangerous power. No one can afford to disarm—and we all know it—while an aggressive military power like Red China remains outside a disarmament agreement. But if Red China were in the United Nations, if its point of view were on record, if it were bound by the same agreements as the other nations, if the peoples of the world were in a position to watch the choices the Chinese make, to see what they are doing, to hear what they are thinking, world opinion could be rallied on the side of peace.

I often wonder if the American people recognize the enormous impact of the United Nations on world opinion. This is the one body in the world where people of all nations and all shades of opinion can be heard, where problems can be discussed, where ways and means of handling them can be thrashed out. One of the chief reasons why the Soviets fear the United Nations and have, as Khrushchev demonstrated so dramatically, attempted to destroy its efficiency, is that when a man states his position in this place his voice is heard everywhere. His actions and his ethics and his motives are judged by peoples in every country. The obstructionist tactics of the Soviet delegates have caused them great loss of prestige among nations whom they hoped to influence by heavy barrages of propaganda.

In my opinion, every nation in the world should be admitted to the United Nations *for the protection of all.* For some years I have been bitterly attacked by people who called me a Communist because I advocate the admission of Red China to the United Nations. An editorial, this past summer, referred to my "friends, those thieves and murderers." The word *Communist,* of course, has become a rallying cry for certain people here just as the word *Jew* was in Hitler's Germany, a way of arousing emotion without engendering thought.

Those who oppose the admission of Red China take as their favorite point of view: "Look at the trouble we have with the Soviets and their continual *Nyet.* Naturally Red China and Russia will always vote together. They stand for the same thing."

But is this true? The increasing conflict of interest between the two great Communist nations, each of whom is constantly attempting to extend its sphere of influence, has become more and more apparent, in spite of friendly speeches occasionally made by their respective leaders.

One thing seems obvious to me. You can't fight Communism anywhere by pretending that it isn't there. And yet a portion of our country is still trying to do this. I can understand that these people feel that Communists give only lip service to many of the beliefs of the United Nations, and the resolutions passed by it. But even lip service is a help. Certainly when people are put in a public spot where they are exposed to world opinion and where they have to work with people of different points of view, it is bound in the end to broaden their outlook.

The main reason for looking realistically at the question of universal membership to the United Nations, the main reason for trying to influence Red China so that she will wish to join, is that every nation will eventually have the knowledge of nuclear fission. The only eventual security against nuclear weapons is disarmament. We cannot contemplate any kind of peace machinery that leaves out 650,000,000 militant people. Bluntly, to leave Red China outside such control agreements would be to give them control of whatever part of the world they want. A single great power left outside a disarmament agreement could determine the course of the whole world if it wished. This is the inescapable truth.

The United Nations is not a club of congenial people; it is, as it should be, a reflection of the whole world, with its turmoil, its conflicting interests, its diverse viewpoints. There has been a great deal said in certain areas of our country about the value of a council of nations all of whom think more or less alike. Mr. Herbert Hoover recently made a speech in which he suggested that we add a council of free states to function with the United Nations to preserve peace in the world. Here we find a failure to see that in the United Nations itself a revolution has been going on. Conditions have changed from the time when it was originally conceived. It is preposterous for us to believe that there are nations which would consent tamely to being left out of any matter that affects the world as a whole.

Frequently one encounters people who feel that there should be no more Communist nations in the United Nations, which would make nonsense of the whole UN concept. I wonder if they have ever added up the votes in the United Nations. So far as I can recall, the majority has always been against the Communist nations. What on earth are these people afraid of? How much faith do they have in the strength of their own cause?

In earlier days there was much fear that the emerging young nations in Africa would not be able to function satisfactorily in the United Nations, that they would have little if any interest in international questions. At first, this fear seemed justified. There was a tendency among certain groups to vote as a bloc, and to vote solely in the interests of African questions. But while the United Nations is serving as a forum for world opinion, it is also serving another purpose that few people appear to recognize. It is one of the most important schools in the world.

Over and over, I have watched the arrival of new delegates from new nations, which have only recently acquired their freedom from colonial rule. Now a fight for freedom in a nation is a domestic matter. When the delegates arrive here their interest is concentrated exclusively on their domestic problems. They have no interest whatever in the world outside. And here, I might point out, we are in no position to criticize. For many, many years after our own revolution, the American people remained stubbornly aloof from the world and a small nucleus still does so!

But I have studied the votes of these African representatives. Within an unbelievably short time, usually before the end of the first year, something happens to the point of view of the new delegate. For months he has been listening to the discussion of world problems. And he learns that the problems of his own country, like those of other nations, are not merely domestic in their scope. All of them have international repercussions, whether it is a matter of education, or the growing and acquiring of food, or the importation of machinery, or the building of dams. So the delegate learns to think, literally, like a man of the world.

Adlai Stevenson said not long ago: ". . . the peculiar merits of multilateral aid programs under United Nations auspices are being recognized more widely than ever. This is especially true in the new nations of Africa. I am told that the delegates to the recent meetings of the United Nations Economic Commission for Africa in Addis Ababa, were unanimous and emphatic in their desire to see the United Nations become a major partner in their development program."

One great strength of the United Nations is often not recognized; indeed, it is often regarded as a weakness. That is the amount of talk that goes on. Now the value of a public forum where people can protest their wrongs is enormous. In the first place, they are able to bring their problems and their complaints before world opinion; to arouse wide discussion about how their problems can be solved. But the second advantage is that talk is a wonderful way of letting off steam. It is a kind of safety valve. As long as men are arguing about the situation in words, they are not trying to solve it with bullets.

This reminds me of the conclusion of a very long talk which I had with Mr. Khrushchev in Russia, in the course of which we discussed a great many problems on which we were far apart. I can't, indeed, recall any point of agreement. When we parted he asked whether he could tell the press that it had been a friendly meeting.

"You can tell them," I suggested, "that we agreed to disagree."

"At least," he pointed out, "we weren't shooting at each other."

As long as talk goes on—at least we aren't shooting at each other.

It is up to every one of us as individuals to see what can be done, step by step, to create a climate of peace and to provide machinery for keeping it. Here, I feel, there is an urgent need for the women of America to work to strengthen the United Nations and to spread information about it, its functioning, its value, among the people of the country.

We should arouse public opinion to demand that, as far as possible, we work through the United Nations as part of a world team in dealing with foreign nations, and not by-pass it to act on our own.

Not long ago, I was talking with some of the women peace marchers. I said that I could understand why our youngsters wanted to demonstrate outside the White House. For those who were too young to vote this provided their only outlet, their only chance to express their opinions. But it seemed to me a futile action for grown women, a complete waste of energy.

Why, I asked them, instead of expending their energy in this pointless fashion, did they not devote it to trying to think out the first step we could take toward peace? *Because every step taken toward peace is a good step.*

One such step has occurred to me. It has been my experience that whenever I talk to foreign delegates they say: "You Americans do not really want a peaceful world and disarmament. If you stopped manufacturing munitions you would have a financial disaster. Your economy depends on war production, on not having peace."

Now they have a legitimate point. If we are going to convince the world that we are not merely paying lip service to the idea of disarmament, we must be able to answer this criticism satisfactorily. This means that it is our job, as individual citizens, to begin to educate our executives and our government representatives. We can call on them either at home or in Washington. We can suggest that the time has come, in this area as in others, to deal with the problem *by planning ahead.*

We might suggest that the President call a meeting of leaders in industry and labor and say to them something like this:

"Gentlemen, we must be prepared for disarmament. Let us together, or you by yourselves if you prefer, plan for such a situation. What would you convert to? How long would it take? What would you expect the government to do in the way of tax reduction or, perhaps, the retraining of labor in new skills?

"You labor people must think things through, too. Under automation, you must be aware that the workers will have to be better educated, more highly skilled. You must discuss this with industry and with government to see what can be done to prepare the worker for a peaceful world and industry for production without war contracts."

If this kind of thinking and planning were being done today we would be able to answer our doubting friends with perfect assurance. We could then tell them, "We have a plan. We know exactly what we will do and how long it will take and what it will require. So you see we do mean what we say when we talk about disarmament."

This would make clear to the Soviets, too, whose distrust of us is as deep as ours of them, that we are really devoted to the concept of world peace.

Certainly this is a positive first step, of more value than parading before the White House. Every such step is worth all the speeches and the gestures and the shoe banging in the world.

While we are appealing to industry, labor, and government in this country to plan for conversion to peaceful manufacture, we could go a step farther and carry the whole problem to the United Nations. We could explain what we have in mind, and how we plan to implement peace. We could ask the delegates from other nations: "How many of you will do this?"

This would be a direct challenge to the Soviets, who would have to face world opinion if they rejected the plan, and make clear that their propaganda about the warmongering Americans is utterly untrue.

A decision on our part to plan for conversion of defense manufacturing would have an impact on the neutral nations, particularly on those who get military assistance from us. We would have to tell them: "You understand that if we carry this plan through we must, of course, cut off our military aid to you. Can you prepare for this change in your own country?

What kind of economic aid would you need to replace our defense material?"

People constantly ask how we can help to strengthen the United Nations. The way to do this is to strengthen our support here at home and to show by example that we are trying to live up to the ideals established by the organization. Our Bill of Rights is really the basis for the Universal Declaration of Human Rights but, as we know, we have not yet succeeded here at home in proving ourselves staunch advocates of civil liberties and equal rights for all human beings throughout the country. We must correct this situation if we are going to have something better than pure materialism to offer the world, something the Soviets can never offer because it is contrary to their whole system.

We have to work with the people as they are in this country, with all their shortcomings. But if we walk with heads erect and fight for the things we believe in, example will somehow affect every other nation as well as our own future and that of our children.

I remember clearly my husband's words in his last State of the Union address in 1945: ". . . in a democratic world, as in a democratic nation, power must be linked with responsibility and obliged to defend and justify itself within the framework of the general good."

9.

THE INDIVIDUAL IN THE REVOLUTION

> The timidity of our public opinion is our disease, or, shall I say, the publicness of opinion, the absence of private opinion.
>
> RALPH WALDO EMERSON

Some time ago, Adlai Stevenson commented with some alarm, "We are not in danger of becoming slaves any more but of becoming robots." Justice Douglas referred to the same condition when he spoke of what he called "the American sickness," the end of the free and courageous use of the mind.

A democracy is made up of one man and one and one and— *ad infinitum*. But each man is responsible for what he does.

Government is people. The ultimate triumph of the democratic system depends on the individual use of democratic principles. We are not a faceless mass. As individuals we can influence our government at every level. But we must accept this responsibility. We must know what we think and speak out, even at the risk of unpopularity. In the final analysis, a democratic government represents the sum total of the courage and the integrity of its individuals. It cannot be better than they are.

I stress this because of the growing tendency among Americans today, men and women, college boys and girls, to evade personal responsibility, to skirt the necessity of making a choice, to hesitate at expressing an opinion, to take comfort in being part of the herd.

This fear of personal responsibility and of an individual's obligations to himself, his community, and his world provides one of the most alluring baits the Communists hold out to people who are perfectly willing to surrender their freedom for the sake of security—and irresponsibility. Wherever we find this growing tendency toward apathy, we ought to fight it tooth and nail. There could be no more destructive quality for America and its way of life.

It is easy to be a robot. You do not have to think for yourself. You do not have to take a decisive stand. You can allow those about you to influence or shape your point of view. You can accept their ideas and opinions without any critical study.

I have a feeling that we have not sufficiently developed in our people the habit of analyzing a situation, of analyzing people's words, of coming to their own decisions. I think it would be of great value if in our universities we gave the techniques of analyzing a subject from every point of view. It would be sound preparation for coping with world questions, which we must eventually solve. We cannot blindly leave them to government. We are the government.

We have to take a new look at ourselves, at what our kind of government requires of us, at what our community needs from us; and then prepare to take a stand. In the long run there is no more liberating, no more exhilarating experience than to determine one's position, state it bravely, and then *act boldly.* Action brings with it its own courage, its own energy, a growth of self-confidence that can be acquired in no other way. Today we need to be our own Patrick Henrys, calling for action.

For a great many years, certainly for well over seventy-five, the United States has been functioning in larger and larger group structures. This has been useful in many ways; it has played an important part in our development. At the same time, the role of the individual has tended to fade out in the larger group picture. Often the status of the individual has depended to a greater or lesser degree on the extent to which he subordinates himself to the group or at least conforms to it.

Not only is the organization man a victim of this trend. In some of the great housing developments each tenant is expected to live and dress and entertain and watch television exactly as his neighbors do.

Long ago, Emerson said, "For nonconformity the world whips you with its displeasure." That can be attested to by anyone who feels impelled to take an unpopular stand. Indeed, it is becoming increasingly difficult for the individual to remember that he is himself a unique human being, and that unless he keeps the sharp edges of his personality and the hard core of his integrity intact he will have lost not only all that makes him valuable to himself but all that makes him of value to anyone or anything else.

In spite of great industrial organizations and large labor unions; in spite of the housing developments and the pressures of various social groups; in spite, above all, of the lure of surrendering one's opinion to that of the group, the individual remains the vital factor in American life. Without the individual as the steering point, nothing can really be accomplished. Look around you at the major improvements in your life, in your world. Each of them grew out of an individual conviction and an individual ability to act upon that conviction.

Now and then I see individuals who are stirred out of their apathy, who see something which needs to be done, something in which they believe wholeheartedly. They set to work with a will. Then something goes wrong. That is when they need to be reminded, "If at first you don't succeed, try, try again."

Obviously, it takes great determination to go on working, year after disappointed and frustrating year, for some reform that seems important to you. As time passes you feel that nothing has been accomplished. But, *if you give up, you are abandoning your own principles*. It is deeply important that you develop the quality of stamina; without it you are beaten; with it, you may wring victory out of countless defeats, after years of what seemed to be hopeless effort.

I learned this when I was quite young. My first introduction to fighting for unpopular causes was when I was eighteen or nineteen. At that time working women were shamefully exploited. They were not allowed to join men's unions, had few of their own, and the men were not particularly interested in improving conditions of work for them. Such advantages as the men were gaining slowly for themselves rarely touched upon the conditions under which the women were laboring.

I will forever be grateful to Rose Schneiderman, who managed to bring together a small group of working women and a group of socially minded women to educate through the Women's Trade Union League. It was Rose Schneiderman who pointed out to me what was wrong in the conditions of work for women at that time. Some of the union women were eager to have all the reforms come at once. They wanted us to fight then and there for complete equality of opportunity for men and women. But to our small group that seemed very far off. All we asked at first was to gain some measure of protection for the working woman.

A few things we did manage to achieve fairly quickly, but there were others which were to take many years. Along the way, we received a very valuable political education.

For instance, there was a bill for which we worked very hard. We were sure we had all the votes we needed. Then we got a shock. We counted the votes. Some of our stalwart supporters had disappeared from the hall. I looked for them high and low.

It was many days before we discovered a little door under the stairs in the Albany capitol. A short time before the vote was to be taken, our supporters, by ones and twos, had drifted out that door. On the other side, the representative of the National Association of Manufacturers had dispensed very good liquid refreshment. We did not get the vote that time.

All this was disappointing but we were not discouraged. It added up to useful experience, annoying as it was. At least we had learned what we were up against. We learned, too, that this question of women was a double-edged sword. The National Association of Manufacturers might oppose improved working conditions for women, but women, none the less, had great power. We discovered in amusement that the last thing that was wanted was to have the women in a district stirred up. We learned to stir them up.

During this period when Mrs. Thomas Lamont and I had

raised money for the mortgage on the Women's Trade Union League clubhouse, we were both working on social conditions in our own community, our own state. But, as so often happens, once individuals have been stirred to action and have created a basic reform, the effects begin to reach out beyond a given state and influence the rest of the country. The individual is the spur to public action.

We are the government. The basic power still lies in the hands of the citizens. But we must use it. That means that in every small unit of government, each individual citizen must feel his individual responsibility to do the best with his citizenship that he possibly can achieve. This is not just a question of voting on primary day or election day but of making up your mind what party you think best represents your own beliefs, then setting out to help the representatives, and using them at every level of government to carry out the ideas you think are sound.

If you believe in the people who are running for office, work in the campaign. It does not make any difference whether you lick stamps or make speeches as long as you do what you can to make your citizenship effective and try to base your opinion on facts, on information you consider valid. Reach out and try to influence as many people as possible to join with you in this active type of citizenship.

Many many years ago Henry George asked Edward L. Youmans what could be done about corruption in New York politics.

"Nothing," Youmans replied. "You and I can do nothing at all. It's all a matter of evolution. Perhaps in four or five thousand years evolution may have carried man beyond this state of things."

This is the philosophy of defeat and it represents a lack of faith in human beings, which means a lack of faith in the democratic processes. We can all do something about corruption in politics and in every sphere of life.

Our trouble is that we do not demand enough of the people who represent us. We are responsible for their activities. If we find that our representatives, at any government level, are showing no desire to lead their constituents, that they are not attempting to come up with new and productive ideas, we must spur them to more imagination and enterprise in making a push into the unknown; we must make clear that we intend to have responsible and courageous leadership.

Quite often it is the negative qualities that cause more trouble than anything else. The deep sin of sloth. The lack of interest. The apathy of the citizen. What you don't do can be a destructive force. The citizen who sees things going wrong in his community and shrugs his shoulders or complains to his neighbors and stops there is partly guilty of the condition. It is in his hands to rectify it. Too often the need for a new ambulance in the community, a fire engine, better street lighting, improved sanitation is neglected because it seems to be nobody's business. In a democracy it is your business.

Democracy requires both discipline and hard work. It is not easy for individuals to govern themselves. This is one of the things that we must make clear here at home because it is the only way—by example, that is—that we can make it clear to the new countries. This is an important lesson for the future of all the new countries. It is one thing to gain freedom, but no one can give you the right to self-government. This you must earn for yourself by long discipline.

Recently my uncle, David Gray, called my attention to Woodrow Wilson's comment on this question of self-government in his *The Place of the United States in Constitutional Development*. "Self-government," he said, "is not a mere form of institution, to be had when desired, if only proper pains be taken. It is a form of character. It follows upon the long discipline which gives a people self-possession, self-mastery, the habit of order and peace and common counsel and a reverence for law which will not fail when they themselves become makers of law: the steadiness and self-control of political maturity. And these things cannot be had without long discipline."

So often I am asked what the average housewife can do to make a contribution to her country and to the peace race. I sometimes wonder if women have any real conception of the extent of the power and the influence they can wield not only in their communities but, little by little, over the whole country.

The average housewife can be a real force in her community. She can join the organizations that represent her ideas, and those that are working for peace, and those that provide a better understanding in the world. She can follow the activities of the representatives of her political party and make sure they are people who are working to prevent war.

Here again, it is interesting to see that in many countries of the world, both old and new, women, working as individuals, are frequently doing far more for their countries than are women in our own land. We have long prided ourselves on the independence of our women and yet we have fewer of them, in proportion, who are taking an active part in shaping the destiny of their country, overcoming its weaknesses, stimulating its growth.

One thing there is no denying. Any change and raising of the standards of civilization can come only from the people within the country itself. Civilization cannot be imposed from without on reluctant people.

In going about the world, visiting in particular the newer countries or those that are making vast changes in their social structure, I have noticed with interest that it was often the women who had been sent to international meetings who had acquired new impetus, new ideas, and were moved by a real desire to achieve results. Their whole perspective had been enlarged and stimulated by the impact of foreign ways and ideas.

I remember a woman in Iran who told me she had been chosen by her Department of Agriculture to try to improve the lives of women in the villages, to show them how to perform their daily chores in better and more efficient ways. Unfortunately, when she attempted to organize women to work in the villages and teach the people new techniques, she encountered an unexpected problem. Either the husbands or the fathers of these women said, "You cannot do this." They were Mohammedans. A woman who came in contact with other men would not be able to marry.

The enterprising woman in Iran was—nearly—defeated. How on earth was she going to find women who would be willing to do this necessary educational work in the villages if conditions were ever to be any better? It was too great a sacrifice to expect a woman to give up forever any idea of having a husband and children.

Then she thought of a group of unfortunate women who, being disfigured, were therefore unmarriageable. These women had nothing to lose and they had a great deal to gain, a productive and useful life. So it was that through the individual efforts of one woman with imagination many people were trained to their benefit and encouraged to want to better themselves. The men were extremely slow to accept the changes, but, influenced by the women who benefited, they have now, I understand, done so.

If a single woman working under such adverse conditions as these can achieve results that are so clearly beneficial and far-reaching, why cannot more of our women spark ideas for improving their communities, their schools, public health, and the standards of local government? Above all, why cannot more of them spark ideas for advancing the cause of peace, on whose triumph our future existence depends?

Example is the best lesson there is. An example of dynamic participation in the life of the community on the part of the women would influence, in many cases, the attitude of the young toward their responsibilities as individuals.

Now and then, I hear complaints that the young have lost all sense of adventure. Not for them the hazards of the people who settled the Plymouth Colony. Not for them the dangerous and rugged trek to the West. Not for them the boldness and self-confidence that led their ancestors to shape their own future.

"Well," some of these young people ask, "how can you expect us to shape our own future? The forces of the world that science has discovered are beyond our control. There's nothing we can do about them."

Some of them have turned to the extreme right, some to the extreme left, but the more common complaint is that they simply do not care.

It is my conviction that there is almost no area of life which we cannot transform according to our own desires if we want something badly enough, if we have faith in it, and if we work for it with all our hearts. It is not too much to say that every bad situation is a result of apathy, of lack of planning, of individuals who think, "After all, it's not my business."

Of course, it is our business, yours and mine. This is our country, our government. These are our representatives. These are our laws. As far back as Jefferson's time, one single vote prevented the abolition of slavery, which would have prevented the tragedy of the Civil War nearly a century later. When a single representative in Congress is able to put through an amendment that prevents us from helping the United Nations financially, and thus hamstrings our only machinery for peace, the last best hope of man, we cannot blame him solely. The absent members who failed to do their job were equally responsible.

The picture of a nation is the sum of the images of all its people; foreign policy embodies all our voices and choices. When we don't like it, we must do something about it, no matter what the risks.

"A lost battle," de Maistre said once, "is a battle one thinks one has lost." But the battle isn't won unless it's your business, unless you care with all your heart that it should be won, unless you hold fast and refuse to panic when the going is rough, unless you reject all attempts to frighten you, unless you refuse to be overwhelmed by any possible dangers that may never arise, unless you remember:

> And in the dark how easily
> Each bush becomes a bear.

The men who founded our government believed that human beings could rise to individual responsibility, that they had the intelligence to govern themselves. We must struggle to give every individual citizen a sense of his or her responsibility not only at home but, in this small new world of ours, abroad.

Sometimes through apathy we allow demagogues in different parts of the nation to lead us by the nose temporarily because we do not realize that self-government requires self-examination, action by the individual, standards, values, and the strength to live up to them.

Wherever we turn we find that our indifference has permitted our weaknesses to exist. Our pockets of poverty did not grow up overnight. They grew because it was nobody's business to wipe them out. Automation, which could be a blessing, looms as a new fear because it is nobody's business to do the kind of planning that would eliminate fear and allow us to profit by new methods.

But, someone will say, how are we going to find the answers to these questions? We must keep on trying, again and again and again. We must hang on one more minute.

Back in the 1930's, when the United States was on the edge of a complete breakdown in its economy, Elmer Davis wrote in *The Saturday Review of Literature:* "To admit that there are questions which even our so impressive intelligence is unable to answer, and at the same time not to despair of the ability of the human race to find, eventually, better answers than we can reach as yet—to recognize that there is nothing to do but keep on trying as well as we can, and to be as content as we can with the small gains that in the course of ages amount to something—that requires some courage and some balance."

PART THREE

TOMORROW

'Tis not the concern of a day, a year, or an age; posterity are virtually involved in the contest, and will be more or less affected, even to the end of time, by the proceedings now.

THOMAS PAINE, *COMMON SENSE*

Those who expect to reap the blessings of freedom must, like me, undergo the fatigues of supporting it.

THOMAS PAINE, *THE CRISIS*

10.

THE LAND IS BRIGHT

I wish I could convey the sense I have of the infinity of the possibilities that confront humanity—the limitless variations of choice, the possibility of novel and untried combinations, the happy turns of experiment, the endless horizons opening out.

ALFRED NORTH WHITEHEAD

Orwell in his *1984* and Aldous Huxley in his *Brave New World* each provided us with an appalling picture of the future of mankind, a life dominated by scientific method in which the humanities and the human spirit had been destroyed. But this picture is obviously based on the astonishing idea that man will supinely let himself be governed by science, not that he will use science as an enlightened tool to make his world closer to a Utopia than man has ever dreamed, still retaining his human dignity as a person and his independence as an individual.

Our choice is not one, as these alarmed novelists appear to believe, of science or the humanities. What we must learn to do is to create unbreakable bonds between the sciences and the humanities. We cannot procrastinate. The world of the future is in our making. *Tomorrow is now.*

Earlier this year, Dr. Glenn T. Seaborg addressed the National School Boards Association. "We must," he said, "face the fact that our population will nearly double by the year 2000. Meeting increased needs for food, homes, education, jobs and recreation will strain our resources to the utmost. We must give urgent attention to problems of farm production, conservation of national resources, replacement of fossil food energy sources with the development of new energy sources such as nuclear energy."

This is a statement which we should read and reread. In less than forty years vast changes will inevitably affect the United States in every area. We must plan now—long-range, farsighted, bold planning to meet the great challenge of the future. The year 2000 sounds remote, faraway. Is it? Let us remember that it will come in the lifetime of people who are thirty years old now.

I have emphasized in this book two areas in which we must begin preparation today: education and the essential need of sparking a new, deep, and fervent sense of responsibility in every individual.

A third area, perhaps the most dramatic because it has become the most prominent in much of our recent thinking, for which we must now begin long-range planning, is in the field of science. Either science will control us or we will control it. That is the sum and substance of the matter. By becoming its master we can build the kind of world we want to have. Nothing can stop us but inaction, lack of imagination, lack of courage, and lack of trained knowledge.

The future is literally in our hands to mold as we like. But we cannot wait until tomorrow. Tomorrow is now. That cannot be repeated often enough.

In the very near future, in some cases even today, we see that an enlightened and imaginative use of scientific knowledge, and a constant extension of that knowledge into the unknown, impinges upon almost every element of our lives. Its effect will be felt in our economy, in the food we eat, in our physical health and well-being.

Science in medicine has already developed radioisotopes which are being used in diagnosis of disease and in therapy as well.

Science reaches out to increase our knowledge of the distant past as well as to help us transform our methods to fit the future. It solves old mysteries of history. (An analysis of a hair from Napoleon's head indicates that he may have died of arsenic instead, as was supposed, of cancer.) It adds depth to our knowledge of the art of the past, and its age, as well as giving us clear evidence of the ways in which long-forgotten people lived and behaved.

Through the new sciences we will have more and more released energy in the form of power. We are only becoming dimly aware of the possibility of this energy for peace, for turning salt water into fresh, for the irrigation of wastelands so as to end the specter of hunger.

Science can not only fling a man into orbit but it can, through Telestar, find new and exciting ways of extending and improving communication throughout the world.

Science can find more and more data on weather so that, in time, we may be able to control its more destructive qualities.

Science may be able to find ways of making the desert bloom, of making it possible to grow crops in soil that has long been worked out and unproductive. It has already begun to increase our knowledge of fertilizers and therefore to increase the food production of the soil. In short, it could feed the whole hungry world.

Science, through automation, can perform the dreary tasks that deaden men's initiative; and it can, if we are intelligent enough to work for it, find new and more rewarding work for the people whom it displaces.

Science can produce power anywhere so that there will be no further need for the monstrous growth of cities.

Science can extend the life of perishable food, such as fish and fruit, so that it can be used over a long period of time and not be wasted in spoilage.

But science, wonderful, inexhaustible as its possibilities are, is not enough in itself. Science is a tool by which men will build their future. The future will depend on man's use of his tool. Ultimately, the basic factor again is the individual, his courage, his responsibility, and his imagination.

I am not afraid of 1984. I believe that, with proper education to enable us to master the secrets of science, with a strong sense of responsibility for our own actions, with a clear awareness that our future is linked with the welfare of the world as a whole, we may justly anticipate that the life of the next generation will be richer, more peaceful, more rewarding than any we have ever known.

What we do here will influence every part of the world; what happens in every part of the world will influence us. So we are faced by the most difficult problem of all—that of man's dealings with his fellows on a basis of mutual respect and good will.

For instance, in the unsolved problem of the poorer nations, if we do some long-range planning, based on actual needs and on future growth, we will not only stimulate world economy, we will not only build the purchasing power of the poor nations, but we will be building future markets for ourselves.

Our standard of living depends on two major factors: the growth of new markets and the substitution of new substances to take the place of our dwindling natural resources.

I do not feel that we have been particularly intelligent in this respect. Our economic aid, in particular, does not seem to be achieving its purpose. In almost every new country there are natural resources which we need, and will need increasingly, in our own production. Why do we not study this situation, help develop the things we need, and buy them? We would help the economy of the new country and our own at the same time, stimulating a flow of money both ways. This is sound economics. It is also sound common sense.

Finally, if we are to build this genuinely Brave New World, which lies within our grasp, we must remember the key word *brave*. We must learn to cast out crippling fear. How strange it is that we all seem to be afraid of one another!

I recall an amusing occurrence that happened on a recent July the Fourth; I was asked to receive the Soviet cultural attaché and his party at Hyde Park. I pointed out that the visit would take place on July the Fourth but I was assured that this did not matter.

I followed the custom of many years. There was a picnic for all the young people and after lunch I read aloud the Declaration of Independence and the Bill of Rights, explaining the background and the reason for each of these safeguards to our personal freedom. I was aware that this could not be very palatable to my Russian guests.

Later, they asked to visit the Franklin D. Roosevelt Library and we started out in my car. I had forgotten the annual July the Fourth parade in Hyde Park so we were held up at a crossroads while it passed.

The Russians had been indoctrinated, of course, with the image of a warmongering America, so on this, our great national holiday, they apparently expected to see such a display of military strength as might be seen on a national holiday in the Red Square.

A group of people went by in uniform.

"Military?" my guests asked.

"Boy Scouts," I explained.

Another group marched by in uniform.

"Military?" they asked again.

"The volunteer fire department," I said.

At length a car went by. Four middle-aged war veterans, who had been stuffed into uniforms they had long grown too stout to wear in comfort, were driven past.

"Military," I said triumphantly.

Long ago, there was a noble word, *liberal*, which derives from the word *free*. Now a strange thing happened to that word. A man named Hitler made it a term of abuse, a matter of suspicion, because those who were not with him were against him, and liberals had no use for Hitler. And then another man named McCarthy cast the same opprobrium on the word. Indeed, there was a time—a short but dismaying time—when many Americans began to distrust the word which derived from *free*.

One thing we must all do. We must cherish and honor the word *free* or it will cease to apply to us. And that would be an inconceivable situation.

This I know. This I believe with all my heart. If we want a free and a peaceful world, if we want to make the deserts bloom and man grow to greater dignity as a human being—WE CAN DO IT!

I would like to conclude with these words of Dr. Reinhold Niebuhr: "Nothing that is worth doing can be achieved in a lifetime; therefore we must be saved by hope. Nothing which is true or beautiful or good makes complete sense in any immediate context of history; therefore we must be saved by faith. Nothing we do, however virtuous, can be accomplished alone. Therefore we are saved by love."

My partner, Judy Beck, encouraged me to do this and proofed every draft I wrote. Those who know me know all that entailed . . . and she didn't complain when I woke up in the middle of the night to rewrite or asked her to proof the copy once again. No one could ask for more support or more devotion.

When I asked President Bill Clinton if he would write the foreword, it didn't take him three seconds to say yes. I thank him for his instant support, his foreword, but most of all I thank him for the compassionate, innovative leadership he gives to billions of people around the world. Like ER, he would rather light a candle than curse the darkness.

As for the dedication, Hillary Rodham Clinton and Melanne Verveer are the leaders of my lifetime. They give me courage, determination, strength, skill, grit, and laughter—all that we need to change the world.

ALLIDA BLACK

Acknowledgments

Bringing Eleanor Roosevelt's final call to action back into print has been a joyous process involving a splendid team of colleagues and friends. It gives me great pleasure to thank them.

Nancy Roosevelt Ireland, executor of Eleanor Roosevelt's literary estate, secured the copyright permission necessary to bring *Tomorrow Is Now* back into print. She answered e-mails on vacation, late at night, and with unfailing grace and good humor. We had been longtime colleagues, but this process made us friends.

My agent and high school classmate, Anna Olswanger, handled the auction and my excitement with aplomb.

Harvey Kaye, a true Rooseveltian in spirit and in scholarship, read drafts, listened to me obsess about the points I had to omit, and helped me say what I wanted to say within the word limit Penguin Classics set for the introduction.

Elda Rotor of Penguin Classics "got it" from the start and did all she could to expedite publication. I think ER would have enjoyed writing for her.

Maeve Kelly and Kathleen Cooper critiqued the introduction and made me laugh while they did it. Richard Schwartz insisted, in his own inimitable fashion, that I state clearly and boldly why this book is so important and, in the process, made me even more determined to see *Tomorrow Is Now* reissued.

William J. vanden Heuvel, Ann Lewis, and Beth Newburger model Rooseveltian behavior each second they walk the earth. Their dedication to the Roosevelts is unparalleled. To be their friend and colleague is one of the high honors of my life.